WHO AM I?

WHO AM I?

Identity in the Age of Consumer DNA Testing

ANITA KATHY FOEMAN

West Chester University

BESSIE LEE LAWTON

West Chester University

cognella®

SAN DIEGO

Bassim Hamadeh, CEO and Publisher
Todd R. Armstrong, Publisher
Tony Paese, Project Editor
Alia Bales, Production Editor
Abbie Goveia, Graphic Design Assistant
Stephanie Kohl, Licensing Coordinator
Natalie Piccotti, Director of Marketing
Kassie Graves, Senior Vice President of Editorial
Jamie Giganti, Director of Academic Publishing

Cover images:
Copyright © 2017 Depositphotos/SvyatLipinskiy.
Copyright © 2013 iStockphoto LP/ImageSource.
Copyright © 2013 iStockphoto LP/drbimages.
Copyright © 2018 iStockphoto LP/MangoStar_Studio.
Copyright © 2018 iStockphoto LP/brusinski.
Copyright © 2019 iStockphoto LP/AlexanderFord.
Copyright © 2019 iStockphoto LP/AnnaStills.
Copyright © 2019 iStockphoto LP/maroke.
Copyright © 2019 iStockphoto LP/alvarez.
Copyright © 2020 iStockphoto LP/LaylaBird.

Printed in the United States of America.

cognella® | ACADEMIC
PUBLISHIN
3970 Sorrento Valley Blvd., Ste. 500, San Diego, CA 921

BRIEF CONTENTS

CONTENTS

INTRODUCTION

Have you ever wondered about the origins of your family? Are you curious about your ethnicity or race? Have you heard or told stories about your family's past? Would you like to know the science that can help to uncover some of these mysteries?

DNA testing is a scientific way to explore these questions. Everyone has a unique combination of DNA molecules in their cells. They form a genetic blueprint, providing insights into your ethnic heritage. But many people don't know what their DNA says (and does not say) about them; and many are surprised when they find out.

Genealogist Donald Panther-Yates and his coauthor, marketing professor Elizabeth C. Hirschman, write that the test results of direct-to-consumer DNA kits may be a "transformation in the way that race and ethnicity are conceived and acted on in the popular consciousness."[1] Genetic information can reinforce what is known and acknowledged in family lore. Other times, it can challenge or even upend known accounts. Our goal with *Who Am I?* is to show how people use these test results to undertake a process of negotiating identity, shaping and informing how we see ourselves (a personal identity) and how others see us and the relationship between ourselves and others (social identity).

We see this moment as an opportunity to talk about the mis/conceptions about race, culture, and ethnicity in a fresh way, one that begins with a belief that we are all amazing human specimens. We want to reinforce that what connects us is greater than what divides us.

A Little About This Book

The foundation of this book is the most comprehensive research on DNA and identity construction in the field of communication studies. Back in 2006, the DNA Discussion Project was established

---

1   Hirschman & Panther-Yates, 2008, p. 64.

at West Chester University in Pennsylvania to conduct research in how results of direct-to-consumer DNA tests were expanding, changing, and contesting students' identity perceptions of themselves. Since that time, more than 3,000 people have participated in the project. We write more about the DNA Discussion Project in Chapter 1, and additional information can be found on the project's website (www.wcupa.edu/DNADiscussion) and in popular media and social media coverage that we have sprinkled at the end of each chapter. Just scan the QR codes at the end of each chapter to learn more about the project.

Chapters 1 and 2 cover the nature of identity, what constructs it, and how DNA results can change these perceptions and narratives. Chapters 3 and 4 examine how one's identity can be contested, be that by lived experiences, social attitudes, or DNA results. In the next two chapters we apply sample perspectives and theory to several case studies: Chapter 5 looks at people who find unexpected ancestry (that uncover family secrets); Chapter 6 presents cases of people who hope to be part of communities to which they are not necessarily genetically connected. Chapters 7, 8, and 9 explore the issues of intersectionality (how do your different identities interplay), the ethics surrounding consumer DNA testing, and what is potentially new on the horizon.

A Little About Us

At the outset, we as your authors want to acknowledge our perspectives and limitations in this venture; we each come to this conversation from particular backgrounds and research agendas.

Anita Foeman

I'm an African American female who began my academic career examining African Americans in various organizational settings. I then moved on to examine multiracial people and families, which led to this area of research. For me, the link between the genesis of human existence and Africa is clear, and I see this work as an opening to repair some of the disparagement of Black people worldwide. The story of Africa becomes the story of all humanity that is inclusive, in a way that traditional history often was not. It also recasts how we discuss history. The great human migration into Europe, Asia, the Middle East, throughout the Americas, and all parts of the globe includes human conflict, for sure, but we are not defined by it. Culture and discovery become guiding themes rather than hopscotching from war to war as the important milestones of history. Fundamentally, we are exploring human identity in relation to culture in all its manifestations.

Bessie Lee Lawton

I was born and raised in the Philippines. For me, I first came to the conversation of race in America as an immigrant who had to find my place in the social structure of the United States, specifically as an Asian who was surprised by the intensity of racial discourse focusing mostly on Black-White conflict. My research then became enmeshed in issues related to race, seeking to understand the experience of minorities and identity negotiation of multiracial individuals (as these were consistent realities in my life as a person of color and a mother of two biracial children). How human identity affects interpersonal relationships and cultural norms, values, and practices are important issues to consider, as the United States will continue to be more diverse and as technology allows all of us to experience cultures from all over the world.

Now that you know a little about us, let's explore a little about you.

1

THE SELF
What Is Identity?

As I (Anita) was cleaning out my parents' home of 60 years, I discovered that my mother had saved all of my report cards from first grade through high school. What shocked me most is that when I read my first-grade teacher's remarks, they were astonishingly accurate and raw (see Figure 1.1). She wrote, "Anita is extremely nervous—she bites her fingers, nails, collar—and cannot sit still." Later she described me as "disorganized." Ouch. Fact is, I still feel like that anxious, young girl, although I have learned to hide it better. Plus, I am now many other things. I am a college professor, I am a mother, I am a wife. I am also an out-of-the-box thinker and a person who has learned to follow her passion, which is also part of my identity. I have identified as female (today, cisgender female) for as long as I can remember, and at some point I realized that I am African American (at the time, Negro). My

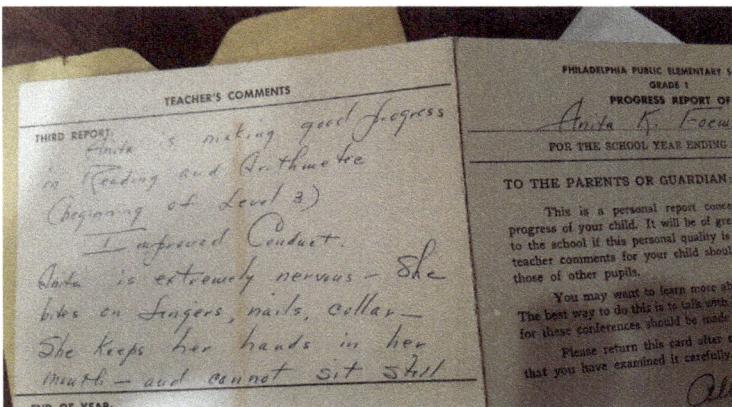

Figure 1.1 Anita Foeman's report card.

identity is multilayered, complex, and evolving.[1] Exploring identity is the work of this book. Soon, you will see that this exploration is framed by one of the newest and most consequential discoveries in modern science, **direct-to-consumer DNA testing**. In our journey, we begin this chapter by asking (a) How will we view identity in the age of direct-to-consumer DNA? (b) How do we begin to manage the infusion of this new information? and (c) What is the DNA Discussion Project that drives this work?

How Will We View Identity in the Age of Direct-to-Consumer DNA Testing?

So, who are *you*? Are you a different person today than you were when you were 6 or 7? Would you be the same person had you grown up in a different family? In a different country? Of a different social class? What elements are fundamental to your sense of self? What if you wore braces to straighten an extremely crooked smile? How about your size or shape? If you gained or lost a large amount of weight or are newly living with a serious illness, are you fundamentally changed? If you changed your racial identification, would you be essentially the same? If you learned something about yourself, some family secret, some new background, would that information change *you*?

These questions are at the core of this book. We focus on the new science of direct-to-consumer DNA as a point of departure. Direct-to-consumer DNA tests allow us to learn about the migration patterns of our ancestors and where they are from. This, of course, is tied to their culture and communication and what we often identify as a person's race or ethnicity. This science has only been available to the wider public for about 15 years, and in the early days, the cost was prohibitive.

In 2006 (when one direct-to-consumer DNA test could cost $450), the DNA Discussion Project at West Chester University (WCU) began exploring identity in the midst of the growing interest in ancestry science. This project is the impetus for this book and our perspective on identity. As we move forward, know that

---

1   Jung & Hecht, 2004.

there is one thing that drives our work and that is important for you to know from the start. *You are a genetic winner.*

Question: What Is in New Direct-to-Consumer Data for Me?

Answer: You Know You Are a Winner!

Have you ever hurried across the street in a rush and looked up to see a car streaking in your direction? Have you ever been in any situation where you thought, "I am lucky that didn't kill me!" Lucky, indeed. Multiply that fortune times 200,000 years since Homo sapiens emerged, or 500 million since the first life slithered out of the ocean. Your ancestors had only to be hit by a car, eaten by a bear, squished by a tree, washed up on shore out of the sea, or any myriad of existential threats, and you would never have come to exist (see Figure 1.2). From a genetic point of view, you have already beaten unimaginable odds. Congratulations.

In our quest for survival, some natural evolutionary changes, **mutations**, that have often helped living beings to adjust to environmental factors, both physical and cultural, also allow **geneticists** to trace our ancestry. But know that when we talk about ancestry, or "race," and the elements that distinguish one group of humans from another, we are talking about a tiny, tiny part of our entire **genome**, about 0.1%. And, as we will see, we can be mistaken about even that small fraction. Still, we are obsessed with it, and it is a defining part of the American culture. And a core part of our identity.

Figure 1.2   Evolution

How Do We Conceptualize Identity?

Our identities, our sense of self, can be a source of inquiry for an entire lifetime. Many elements flow into an identity, and those things can change over time. Our exploration here is one part of that journey, so let's lay out the framework for thinking about identity.

We can think in terms of at least three levels of our identity.[2] The first is our personal identity that would incorporate things like interests and hobbies. This identity relates to things like whether you like haiku or watercolors or hip-hop or jump rope or consider yourself creative or analytical. These qualities relate to you on an individual level and are specific to you. Second, **social identities** are those elements related to our affiliations with groups like an honor society or volunteer club. These uniquely reflect you because they relate to choices you make, associations you select, and how you interact with others.

Third, you probably have cultural identities that more often relate to situations into which you were born and raised. They are usually determined before we make active choices and form the foundation for our outlook in life, often without question.[3] These would include our **ethnicity** and **race**.

New direct-to-consumer DNA tests relate most closely to this formative cultural level of identity, race, and ethnicity, and much of our discussion flows from these factors. But, of course, no two people are alike in terms of how they process their culture through other factors like individual personality, interests, social class, religion, sexual identity, gender, ability, and so on. Further, as we think about the different levels of identity, we often feel a desire to maintain continuity across levels, to avoid what Hecht[4] describes as identity gaps. For example, when you picture an opera lover, do you imagine a person of a certain age, race, social class? If an opera lover does not fulfill those expectations, that person may experience some discord both within and interpersonally. Given all of this, as we move forward, we may relate many factors of identity to race, ethnicity, and

---

2   Spreckels & Kotthoff, 2009.
3   Yep, 2002.
4   Hecht, 1993.

other cultural elements. Let's start with a general comment on how new direct-to-consumer data helps to form identity.

Direct-to-Consumer DNA Reworking Identity Factors

There are quite a few companies that offer direct-to-consumer testing for ancestry. There are several strategies for tracing genetic background. One of the first and most accurate ways to trace ancestry was via mitochondrial DNA (mtDNA). This DNA is found around the nucleus in cells and is not subject to the shuffling and recombination of our typical reproductive chromosomes. MtDNA travels from mother to child, almost exactly intact. Miniscule changes occur only over thousands of years and allow for the ancestry tracking. MtDNA was sequenced long before the full human genome. It is more precise, although more limited in scope, than other ancestry strategies. A male or female can use it to track the maternal line back to deep ancestors and to what are called haplogroups. These are simply groups of genetic similarity.

Obviously, haplogroups can be determined via mtDNA, but also Y DNA, for males. Y DNA (as in the Y male chromosome) tracking is based on the sex-determining chromosome for males in the non-recombining portions of DNA. It is less stable than the mtDNA but can also identify groups of association. Females do not inherit the Y chromosome. So, if a female wants to trace the line from her father to father to father, she would have to begin with a male relative like a brother or her dad.

Haplogroups can also be identified. Haplogroups, from Greek *aplos* (simple) and group, can be maternal (mitochondrial DNA) or paternal (Y DNA). They define genetically similar clusters of people. While haplogroups are very helpful in tracing migration patterns and help us speculate about the origins of human life, they arguably say less about the individual and their health than other ancestry approaches. Haplogroups reflect a more distant line. Still, many people attach very strongly to those lines of identity, and there are plenty of haplogroup chat groups online.

Autosomal DNA is DNA that is the result of the combined DNA from both sides in a person's background. Because this DNA does change and recombine, it is less precise than Y or mtDNA, but many people find it especially interesting because it reflects the

TABLE 1.1 Ethnicity estimate for Anna: Thousands of years ago

AFRICA	23%
Benin/Togo	8%
Nigeria	8%
Ivory Coast/Ghana*	3%
Senegal*	2%
Africa Southeastern Bantu*	1%
Cameroon/Congo*	< 1%

* Low confidence region

full background. People often find it fascinating to see how siblings differ, for example. We get half of our DNA from one biological parent and half from the other, but which half differs from offspring to offspring. The basis of this autosomal work is ancestry informative markers, or AIMs. AIMs come from the variants in our genes—specifically, single nucleotide polymorphisms, or SNPs, a type of genetic variation among people. Each SNP represents a difference in a single DNA building block. And they can be explored in different ways for different purposes.

The most popular tests today are autosomal. A good example of how multiple factors influence how we receive direct-to-consumer DNA information would be in the instances of Anna (see Table 1.1) and Drake, two people who participated in the DNA Discussion Project. Anna only learned of African ancestry in her background as a college student participating in the DNA Discussion Project. Up until then, she had identified as an Asian/European female. As a result, she processed that new identity through decades of opposing information, although she reports that many people have asked her along the way if she is African American. Her response had always been no. Drake, a bit older than Anna, spent a lifetime identifying as a Black male living in the southern United States. When DNA testing revealed that he, like Anna, had 23% or less of African ancestry, their reactions were quite different. Drake, despite his relatively small amount of African ancestry, doubled down on his Black identity, saying "My politics are as Black as night," and he "would always and only be seen as a Black man in America."

Anna responded to her 20-plus percent African ancestry (actually, more than Drake) by seeing it as one part of her identity (albeit "controversial" in her words). Newly incorporating this identity, she explained herself as a "woman of the world," given the many ancestry lines that were part of her profile. Anna is currently raising funds to visit all of the countries that she found in her genetic profile. She describes the experience as "life changing" and expansive. For Anna and Drake, their existing racial, gender, geographic, generational, and other identities intersected with new genetic information. We have found other students of all races who expressed intersections between their racial identity and other factors like social class, geography, and the era in which they live. We also have participants who identify as **biracial** and **multiracial** who are comfortable with that ambiguity.

Race and Ethnicity

We have used the terms *race* and *ethnicity* several times already in this book. These terms, while related, are distinct. Both impact identity. In the general society, race is most associated with phenotype (how we look), or our physical or biological characteristics. We generally assume that certain features are associated with particular geographic origins and genetic profiles (which may or may not be a correct assumption).

Ethnicity classifies people into groups based on common ancestry and shared history, language, and other symbol systems.[5] Like race, these factors can be loose and misunderstood. Race and ethnicity often overlap (but not always) and to different degrees. Gaps between the two identities can be disconcerting for the individual and their co-communicators. For example, an adopted person may have an ethnicity (say, culturally Italian) that seems incongruent with the person's genetic ancestry (for example, Chinese) and may cause dissonance in some settings. Until recently, Americans could make only one choice on the U.S. Census to describe their racial background, and this was intended to capture the entirety of their racial and ethnic classification.[6] Today, Census takers can select as

---

5   Roth & Ivemark, 2018.
6   U.S. Census Bureau, 2010.

many racial categories as they please, and the lines of race are blurring. Latinx respondents are asked two separate Census questions about race and ethnicity. There is even discussion of removing race as an identifier on the U.S. Census altogether.[7]

Direct-to-consumer DNA often reveals new information on geographic associations and adds another layer to what we already know or assume about our backgrounds, creating still more opportunities for ambiguity. It can generate as many questions as it answers. For example, does a person with 4% Asian ancestry have an Asian ancestor three or four generations back, or is this the result of Eastern European ancestors who bordered Europe and Asia? Or something else? Culturally, what might this imply? We have had several participants recall a cultural characteristic in their families (Yiddish expressions, Indian or Italian cuisine, children's stories, etc.) that might be related to a lost past. In other cases, people have large percentages of regions in their background and no family narrative to explain it. It is also important to note that direct-to-consumer DNA test results do not have a 100% accuracy rate, and some ranges for ethnicity estimates can be quite large. Clearly, further investigation is warranted in all cases. Ancestry tracing companies have cropped up offering a variety of genetic tests and insights regarding ethnicities. One must be careful about attaching finality to ethnic breakdowns. One major company, FamilyTreeDNA reports in its blog that

> when ethnicity estimates were first produced by vendors, they tended to resemble the wild west. ... Today, results are becoming more refined and hopefully, more accurate as reference populations grow and become more reliable. ... Ethnicity is the least precise and the least accurate of DNA tools for genetic genealogy. Ethnicity estimates are the most accurate at a continental level. Within continents, like Europe, Asia and Africa, there has been a lot of population movement and intermixing over time making the term "ethnicity" almost meaningless.[8]

---

7   Cohn, 2015.
8   Estes, 2018.

Frankly, a great deal of our mission is to have people simply discuss race and ancestry in more inquisitive, inclusive, and positive ways. These tests are the start of a new exploration, not the end of the trail and certainly not a definitive statement on our racial and ethnic uniqueness.

In viewing how race and ethnicity shape our identity, two perspectives on identity have been debated in both scholarly work and in common understanding. Both have been linked to direct-to-consumer DNA data. They break down broadly into two categories: essentialist and constructed perspectives.

Essentialism

The concept of essentialism originated with Plato, who lived from 428–348 BC, conceiving that natural qualities have a core essence that is constant within a category and different from one category to the next. You *are* the category and it is you—woman, man, and so on. Any variation within one's essence is the result of an imperfect display of the essence. Variation is an aberration or weakness, a poor example of the essence.

Modern essentialism carries on these beliefs and shapes perspectives on race. In her work on essentialism in everyday thinking, psychologist and linguist Naomi Zack says that common thinking about race has an essentialist quality. She found that preschool children and adults from a variety of cultural backgrounds expected people to belong to certain groups that have "an innate basis, stable category membership, and sharp boundaries."[9]

Any time someone says, "You don't act Asian" or Black or gay or blind, or like a girl, you are probably hearing an essentialist argument. There is a way that one is assumed to "naturally" act in these groups. In our own project, for example, one participant found that he had a small percentage of African in his background (the same as several other White test takers). As an adopted person he had not known much about his biological father. His first comment when he learned this new information about his background was, "I heard that my biological father liked basketball."

Critics of the popularity of direct-to-consumer DNA tests argue that direct-to-consumer DNA results support an essentialist

---

9   Zack, 2003, pp. 44–45.

perspective. Some of the ways we discuss our genetic make-up are directly parallel to the ancient perspective presented. It is easy to see how "the genomic revolution carries in its wake a genetic-essentialist worldview in which our genes are viewed not only as determining our behavior and characteristics but as defining our essential nature and identity. In this worldview, we are our genes." The harshest critics fear that there is a eugenic aspect to this work.[10]

There are certainly elements in ancestry reporting that have an essentialist feel; profiles are presented in neat pie charts with detailed geographic regions identified, down to fractions of a percent, suggesting a kind of precision that simply is not possible.

The nonessentialist reality is that all people migrated out of **sub-Saharan Africa** across many geographic regions, separated most often by somewhat porous physical barriers like mountains and rivers. Political boundaries within regions shifted and changed over time, so the names and borders of locations may have changed from what we think of today, making location designations uncertain. Genetic reference pools needed to identify regional comparisons are not perfect. Scientists at different laboratories make different decisions about how various regions will be labeled and which genetic markers will be included and how. The science gets updated and profiles are changed (see Table 1.2). Yet, there is evidence that people share and integrate these ancestry narratives down to the trace details in essentialist ways.[11] And, without a doubt, the intersection of new genetic data and new **gene editing technology** (switching out our original genes) will create more and new ethical questions about race and identity in the near future, though it is hard to know exactly how.

Genetic tests and the current social situation are already bringing controversy and racial tension to the forefront.[12] This can be seen in the postings of White nationalists on group websites. As you can imagine, identifying who qualifies as "White" is crucial in establishing membership in White nationalist organizations. Apparently, a great deal of time is spent debating race within these groups. Postings suggest that the standards for Whiteness are wobbly and contested but ultimately come down to a genetic

---

10 Phelan et al., 2013.
11 Panofsky & Donavan, 2017.
12 Ibid

TABLE 1.2 Ethnicity estimates: Refined and updated

Benin/Togo: Increased by 28%	28%
Cameroon/Congo: Increased by 13%	23%
Great Britain: Decreased by 5%	13%
Ireland/Scotland/Wales: Increased by 10%	12%
Mali: Increased by 8%	12%
Ivory Coast/Ghana: Decreased by 12%	5%
Nigeria: Decreased by 23%	4%
Senegal: Decreased by 10%	1%
Spain (New)	1%
Native American—North, Central, South: Refined from: Native American 1%	1%

standard. One often listed post reads, "If a person looks White and thinks of himself as White and is the kind of person our other members wouldn't mind their sisters marrying—and if we know he is no more than one-sixteenth non-White, we consider him White."[13] The first noteworthy aspect is that the standard for White nationalist membership is apparently being heterosexual and male (i.e. the person "thinks of *him*self" and "*sisters* marrying"), and the other standard is a numerical percentage: "no more than one-sixteenth non-White." By White we assume they mean European. However, there are many aspects involved in the way the term *European* is defined, and White nationalists discuss that obsessively as well. We will unpack that in a later chapter.

More surprising is that as people posted their DNA profiles in order to establish their bona fides, the reactions were perhaps unexpected. When "bad news" (non-European results) were posted, fellow White nationalists were actually often supportive

13 Ibid., p. 14.

and sympathetic. Some rejected the test or tried to reinterpret the results or otherwise support the now "spoiled" identity of the individual.[14] Their opinions often shifted away from a hard essentialist perspective to one based on an attitude or belief system, and a broad **phenotype**. They were reluctant to excommunicate these people from the community in which they all found support. Indeed, research identifies that many White supremacist leaders (similar to pimps, warlords, and mobsters) target not necessarily true believers for recruitment, but rather they seek to indoctrinate troubled, lonely, and fragile individuals looking for belonging. Derik Black, a young man groomed for White nationalism, left the White supremacist community in 2013 and says that what brought him out of his racist mind-set was kindness from people he had disparaged and from whom he had no reason to expect compassion. Essentialism gives way to compassion.

Genetic tests show us that genetic purity is a hard standard for any group and is likely to lead to undesired exclusivity. There are genetic markers that cluster people into geographic groups, but they are few, and there is more diversity within groups than across them.[15] In our research, we rarely find a person with ancestry from one single region. Perhaps these White nationalist groups can take a page from many members of our DNA Discussion Project research. Finding that their profiles were not as singular as expected, many people make comments along the lines of "If I did not know this about myself, what else do I not know?" That is an open door for change.

Constructivist Views

A constructed identity seems more consistent with a communication perspective, and the data, than an essentialist one. Sociologists Berger and Luckmann, who are credited with establishing the notion of a constructed reality, say that "through language an entire world can be actualized at any moment"[16] and interaction is at the core of how we see reality. The world just "is" (you have likely heard the expression "it is what it is") and *we* impose meaning on it. For example, we have had people literally jump for joy upon finding

---

14 Defleur & Goffman, 1964.
15 Witherspoon et al., 2007.
16 Berger & Luckman, 1966, p. 39.

that they have a marker that indicates a little Middle Eastern or European or African, or whatever ancestry in their backgrounds. Others have literally broken down in tears of sadness over the same results. So, it is not the ancestry to which they are responding; it is some constructed idea of what that association means. Some people disparage their results from a certain group and another person takes pride in it.

We construct social expectations and attitudes. From this constructivist perspective, rather than saying, "He doesn't act Asian," one might assert, "If we say that he is Asian, and he acts in a particular way, then Asians, by definition, act that way." If a person is not acting Asian, that person is not a poor example of an Asian; rather, we have poorly constructed the category, at least in this particular instance. Rather than seeking an essential definition, we can seek useful ones. If we are studying income disparity or mass incarceration, a discussion of the social view of race is imperative. If we are deciding who can enjoy basketball, it is not. When existing categories do not work, from a constructivist view, one can reconstruct them. Generally, we construct through action and language. Direct-to-consumer DNA testing, itself a human construction, simply helps highlight how made up our categories are. Throughout this book we will highlight how different direct-to-consumer tests construct ancestry profiles and how we construct meaning around them.

Have *you* ever felt confined by how a category is constructed for you? What does it mean to be manly or womanly, or Black, disabled, or a student or upstanding or … you name it? Perhaps we can rethink those categories. To paraphrase anthropologist Clifford Geertz, humans are animals suspended in webs of significance that we ourselves have spun.[17] Linguist Benjamin Lee Whorf says, "We cut nature up, organize it into concepts, and ascribe significances as we do, largely because we are parties to an agreement that holds throughout our speech community."[18] In other words, we speak things into existence: important, unimportant, race, ethnicity. That being the case, though it is no easy feat or painless, through new information and dialogue we can remake the world. Later in this chapter we will talk about genetic communication counseling as

---

17 Weiland & Geertz, 1982.
18 Whorf, 1940, p. 230.

people grapple with change that can help them reconstruct how they might see their ancestry results.

The idea that race is socially constructed is widely accepted across fields of sociology, psychology, communication, and the like.[19] Practical examples in U.S. history include a person moving from one state to another and suddenly being identified as a different race. In fact, people have petitioned the government to change their racial categorization.[20]

Students who have participated in the DNA Discussion Project argue over whether Jewish (identified in several ancestry tests) is a religion or a race, if Jews are White, if Indians are Asian, and on and on. Scientists who "read" the genetic profiles must grapple with these same issues as well. In terms of DNA, any group of people that is segregated by space over time can be pinpointed by genetic similarity. Groups like the Amish and other genetically isolated groups have unique and very homogenous genetic profiles. So, race is just one way to articulate some genetic similarity, and maybe not always the best.

Michael Hecht's communication theory of identity (CTI)[21] presents a schema for how identity is continually constructed through communication. CTI presents identity in four layers of interpretation: personal, enacted, relational, and communal. Race exists across all of the levels. The personal exists at the individual level. For example, it is not uncommon for a student in an intercultural communication class to say when asked about her racial identity, "If I had to say, I'd say that I see myself as White." Asked about how this identity is enacted or performed, the student might say, "Well, I basically go places where most people are White; I attend a predominantly White place of worship." When asked about her Whiteness in relation to other people of other races, this student might say, "I treat everyone the same, regardless of race." Finally, in terms of defining how the collective, or community, defines the identity, the same student may state, "Honestly, I rarely think about race at all. I just think of myself as a person." When questioned further, the students agree that "I don't think

---

19 Berger & Luckman, 1966; Burr, 1995.
20 PBS, n.d.
21 Hecht, 1993.

of White as an ethnicity like Black or Hispanic, it's just regular, plain, really nothing, not very exciting. Just regular. Just White."

Hecht is especially interested in cases where the different levels of identity are inconsistent, called identity "gaps." For example, the student in the previous example says, "I don't think of White as an ethnicity like Black or Hispanic, it's just regular, plain, really nothing, not very exciting. Just regular. Just White." And on the other hand, when she says that she does think of, say, African Americans through the lens of race, but "I treat everyone the same, regardless of race," she is revealing an inconsistency between how she sees herself and how she sees people of color, who, by her own logic, are not "regular." It is hard to imagine that she would treat or think of people of color as the same as regular White people, then. However, in her daily life, surrounded by people like herself, she may be able to hold this inconsistency at bay. Under scrutiny, the inconsistencies emerge. Now, suppose this same person discovers that she has some percent of African ancestry in her genetic profile, and this makes her feel vaguely "weird." This identity gap, or distinction between levels of identity can cause dissonance that opens up the possibility for dialogue and discovery. The dissonance exposes how we construct identities and the desire, under pressure, to bring the levels in line and a potential willingness to rebuild to eliminate the gaps.

In our project, one young man unexpectedly found 1% (negligible) African ancestry in his profile. This self-described "White guy" happened to be sitting next to two African American students. When he shared his 1% result, the two wanted to joyously high five him. He was visibly uncomfortable. The moment did not seem appropriate to probe, but it would have been interesting to ask what thoughts and feelings he had at that second. It would be interesting to note if this experience created a gap in his identity (as with the hypothetical student) and if this interpersonal moment opened a door for a new construction of race. Might some of his conceptions of what it means to be African American shift if, in some people's construction of race (even his own) he is African American? Is he still a "regular guy"? Could someone with African ancestry be a "regular" guy, like himself?

The key point is that identity is formed and reformed through interplay among all of the interrelated levels that evolve over time.

Fundamentally, identity is created, maintained, and modified through communication and new information. The dissonance created when gaps appear may provide an opening for dialogue and reconsideration of the concept of race. Such reconsideration may be related to our well-being. According to Jung and Hecht,[22] discrepancies or inconsistencies between or among the four identity layers can create tensions or stress for people. Similarly, previous research has found that "identity gaps contribute to low communication satisfaction as well as ... to more pervasive negative health outcomes such as stress and depression."[23]

How Do We Begin to Manage the Infusion of This New Information?

We can learn to manage in this new era by turning to the techniques of genetic counseling, and we will also introduce you formally to the DNA Discussion Project that works with people to explore the implications of direct-to-consumer DNA data.

Communication Counseling on Genetics

Given the centrality of race and ethnicity to identity, the importance of race and ethnicity in society, and the possibility for anxiety and stress when gaps and other challenges occur across levels of identity, it is relevant to share a therapeutic perspective in managing new ancestry information. The perspective presented here is offered by scholars in family communication in the context of genetic counseling.

Let us first say that in our work on direct-to-consumer DNA and identity we understand that we are not therapists. In all participant consent forms we direct participants to seek the support of professional counselors if they experience distress. However, we do think that it is relevant to approach this project with sensitivity and awareness that these topics have an impact on people.

Because there is no literature that specifically speaks to counseling about direct-to-consumer DNA tests, we turn to the literature

---

22 Jung & Hecht, 2004.
23 Hecht & Lu, 2014, p. 226.

on communication genetic counseling that has long been dedicated to sharing information about disease risk based on genetic tests for an individual or potential offspring. Very similar to ancestry, scientists, counselors, and recipients struggle with how to use data to develop a workable and useful health narrative.[24] Many similar elements apply in genetic counseling as direct-to-consumer DNA testing (although the physical risks for the latter are generally not as consequential). In genetic counseling, first, because genetic information is interpreted by humans and because genes, in some cases, are not destiny, having an identified genetic marker for a disease does not guarantee that a person will develop a genetically linked illness. Genes also do not tell us when a disease might present or how disruptive it might be, and some conditions are not related to just a single gene or gene mutation. All of this means that the recipient has to live with a great deal of ambiguity. Second, results of a genetic test for one individual have implications for the entire family. So a person faced with new DNA health data has to make decisions about sharing the information as well as internalizing it. This information can be interpreted in different ways, depending on the family style.[25]

Professional genetic counselors[26] tell us that families may think in terms of genetic absolutes ("I am going to get this disease and die"), possibilities ("I have a higher risk"), or complete dismissal ("What do they really know?"). In each case, the information may be viewed as a burden, a gift, or a neutral event. Scientific information is continuously being updated and is sometimes speculative (remember discussions of the "gay" gene?) Therefore, learning genetic information sometimes creates as many questions as it answers. Genetic counselors are currently turning to the reciprocal engagement model (REM) in counseling, even referencing the work of Berger and Luckmann[27] on social construction of reality.

Looking at the five tenets of REM[28] in genetic counseling can help us understand the approach. REM places genetic information in the context of a larger counseling relationship and guides the

---

24 Gaff & Bylund, 2010.
25 Koerner et al., 2010.
26 Ibid.
27 Berger & Luckman, 1996.
28 McCarthy et al., 2007.

genetic counselor to (a) share genetic information with clients, (b) create an open and honest relationship in counseling, (c) respect the autonomy of the recipient of the information, (d) assume the resiliency of the recipient, and (e) assume that emotions matter.

In a society with the racial history of the United States, some of the same factors (albeit to a lesser degree) may be relevant when talking about the genetics of race. Living with uncertainty, determining how to share information, and deciding how and how much of the information will be accepted are themes that ancestry DNA testing presents.

We take participant well-being seriously in our DNA Discussion Project. Our consent form clearly states that participants who find DNA results upsetting should seek professional counseling services, and this has happened in some cases. Although participants agree that we may use their names, images, stories, and profiles in our work, we avoid linking information that may embarrass or over-expose individuals. In this book we change some of the details (gender, name, etc.) to provide a level of anonymity. We do not show participants' faces without specific permission.

We tell participants what laboratory we are using to process their DNA. We post the lab privacy statement and inform participants that they can reach out to the lab for additional information. We do most often have ancestry profiles come directly to us as the researchers and then we forward ancestry data to participants, since that is the core of the research project. Upon request, we can give participants access to their genetic links, but linking to genetic relatives is not part of our research and training program. Finding unexpected relatives is an important experience for some of our participants but is not directly relevant to this conversation. Participants can access information about the test easily, and we generally include only people age 18 or older, except for one specific research project that did include minors. In this case, we received consent from the young person and a parent. We include contact information for the University Institutional Review Board and clearly state that participants may withdraw from the project at any time, although their images and ancestry profiles may already be in the public realm and we cannot retrieve the information. The project maintains a webpage with additional information about our publications and work overall. Through these measures, we hope that we meet the goals of (a) sharing information with participants, (b) creating an open and honest relationship with our participants (c) respecting the autonomy of each participant, (d) assuming participant resilience with self-determination, and (e) attending to potential emotional impact.

What Is the DNA Discussion Project?

We have mentioned the DNA Discussion Project several times. Let us explain exactly what the DNA Discussion Project is. In 2006, I began a program of research intended to explore the influence of new ancestry DNA data on racial and family narratives. Over the course of the next 14 years, more than 3,000 individuals have been tested using a basic approach: (1) pre-interview individuals about their known family/racial background, (2) test their ancestry DNA, (3) share their DNA findings with them, and (4) post-interview them to determine how they integrate the new information. The sample is about two thirds female, and a majority belong to the traditional college age range, although we have participants from age 8–70-plus range. Approximately 80% of the sample identify as White, 12% as Black and African, and the rest are a combination of Asian, Latinx, Native American, multiracial, and other. Almost the entire sample is from the mid-Atlantic region, and we have a couple hundred volunteers from the public who have joined the project. DNA samples are taken from a simple noninvasive saliva sample. DNA results are reported as percentages of various geographic regions, such as Africa, Europe, and Asia. Further, the broad categories were subdivided to indicate more specific areas within a region, such as Italy/Greece, Ivory Coast/Ghana, and Spain.

The DNA Discussion Project began with a small grant from the Multicultural Faculty Commission at West Chester University, offering funding for people who wanted to explore diversity in unique ways. I had always been fascinated by the mapping of the human genome, long before its completion in 2000. In 1987 when an article came out in the journal *Nature* announcing that it was possible to identify not just a figurative, but a literal mitochondrial Eve who traced back to sub-Saharan Africa, it was exciting. Later, when the first draft of the "Human Genome" was completed on

June 26, 2000, my interest was heightened. Then, when I saw reports of the work of geneticists like Bryan Sykes[29] and Spencer Wells,[30] who began to talk about the likelihood of revealing our individual ancestral lines via DNA analysis, I jumped at the opportunity to explore the possibilities. Suppose we could ask people what they think about their racial background and then ancestry DNA test them and compare the two "stories" and their reactions. What would happen? It was certainly a novel idea at the time. I had trouble locating a laboratory to run the test. Most people I approached had no idea what I was talking about, but I did finally find a lab that charged $450 for each test. I applied for and received a grant for $1,500 to test three undergraduate student volunteers. One participant identified as White, one as Black, and one as biracial (White and Black). I was off. The early days were like the Wild West. In fact, in those early days one lab went out of business (with $10,000 of grant funds!); others sent back lists of numbers and locations that seemed random and difficult to decipher.

One lab even more recently used a strange algorithm that was problematic and based identification on a combination of factors to identify "Latino" as a category. With the help of our genetic specialist at West Chester University, Dr. Leslie Slusher, I was able to wade through the data and consider what it did and did not reveal. In the early days, error ranges were very large, and there was little agreement on the best way to present the information to the general public. Terms like haplogroups, SNP, SNR, mitochondrial DNA, and derivative categories like Latino (not a geographic region) were used, and other complex technical factors made understanding difficult for anyone not in the sciences. Still, each of my first three participants found among the list of geographic ancestral regions, places that they would not expect in their backgrounds. The data I received in pre and post interviews was rich. And the participants were excited to be involved, so in that regard the early work was a success.

I also tried to educate myself by reading approachable works like Bryan Sykes's *Seven Daughters of Eve* about the beginnings of this ancestry genetic work and more recently Siddhartha Mukherjee's

29 Sykes, 1998.
30 Wells, 2006.

The Gene: An Intimate Story.[31] I attended several classes on campus where the genetics relevant to my work was being taught. I also attended a session for high school biology teachers at the Dalton DNA Learning Center in New York where I was able to isolate a DNA segment. I was goofy excited next to about a dozen hardened high school biology teachers who were giving up their Saturday to get the continuing education credits required for their ongoing certification. I was pleased that my isolated DNA segment came out the best!

My work seemed in sync with the discussions about race and its social construction that were and are ongoing in society, and I was able to publish my first paper "Science and Magic: DNA and the Racial Narratives that Shape the Social Construction of Race in the USA" in 2006. All that being said, I feel that I still do not know enough about the genetics of race, and I am sure that I never will. I am also continually finding new aspects of the discussion of the social construction of reality.

Current Status

In 2011, Dr. Bessie Lawton, a co-researcher with whom I had been conducting research on multiracial families, joined the project. Working together, we established a research protocol that allowed us to explore and examine a wider range of variables using both quantitative and qualitative ways and allowed us to look for patterns in our data. These approaches took the project to the next level, and we have been able to conduct research focusing on different groups, questions, and methodologies. For example, we have looked at biracial/multiracial individuals and tried to answer questions specifically relevant to the Black/White dichotomy. Over the years, we have also collaborated with other researchers and practitioners from diverse fields, such as Dr. Randall Rieger, a statistician in the university's Math Department, social psychologists and biologists from other universities, and an artist from New York.

---

31 Mukherjee, 2016.

A Word on Privacy and Accuracy

When we talk about the DNA project, the two concerns that almost always come up relate to the accuracy and privacy of data generated. These topics are addressed more fully in Chapter 8, but let us mention this initially here. Since the completion of the Human Genome Project over 70 companies now provide ancestry testing.[32]

In terms of accuracy, the basic strategy used in these tests is to track natural genetic mutations that take place over time as humans moved out of Africa and traversed the globe, settling in groups in various places. These ancestral roots go back hundreds of years. Tests compare your genes to a database of people from different places in the world. The federal government's 1,000 Genomes Project ran between 2008 and 2015, creating the largest public catalogue of human genetic data to support research, especially medical research. The final phase of the project was able to complete the genetic sequence for more than 2,500 people from 26 distinct world populations. Much of the direct-to-consumer testing today is based on this work.[33] Depending on what any particular individual inherited, the genetic profile that is generated may reflect the path of your ancestors more than how you identify today. In any case, the larger the company's database the better the chances of an accurate match for you specifically. The larger the percentage, the more likely the match is an accurate representation for you. People will sometimes ask, "How far back does this go?" Think in terms of what you inherited. You might inherit a characteristic from many generations back, or some ancestral element may be lost in the genetic shuffle. You inherit basically half of your genes from each biological parent, but which half? This is why siblings can have different genetic profiles.

Also, remember, if you belong to a group that is not in the database, the analysis can only do its best to get you as close to your group as possible. Each company has its own test, and each company decides what genes to include and how to label them. The largest, most credible companies tend to give similar results. Companies may update from time to time as the science improves and their databases grow. The large companies generally update

---

32 Phillips, 2016.
33 1,000 Genomes Project Consortium, 2010.

your data for free. Also, know that the tests are quite good at identifying your "genetic relatives," so you can expect people to reach out to you if you make your profile available to other test takers.

In terms of privacy, each company has its own privacy statement. The larger companies tend to have strong privacy limits. You can generally decide if and how much you want others to see and with whom you want to share your data. Read the privacy statements carefully so you know what you are signing up for. Be aware that if you upload your data to public sites, even for further analysis, you are making your data public.

We have thrown a lot of information at you thus far. In Chapter 2, we move into how all of this complex data is winnowed into stories that become part of our family narrative.

DISCUSSION QUESTIONS

1. Talk about your life when you were in elementary school. How similar is your current identity to that young person? What important events have helped to shape the person you are today?

2. Discuss some way in which a category has made you feel bad about yourself. How do we construct that category that does not work for you? Would you do away with the category or reconstruct it? How?

3. Which do you think is more important in how you identify, genetics or life experience?

4. Would you feel comfortable taking a direct-to-consumer DNA test? Why or why not?

ACTIVITIES

1. Make a list of 15–20 factors that you feel go into your identity.

2. Interview someone else in your class or among your friends regarding an important experience that shaped their identity.

LEARN MORE

Our Common Core: Ancestry DNA-Hope for Humanity

Web Link: https://tinyurl.com/y3b5hpjw

CREDITS
Fig. 1.2: Copyright © 2018 Depositphotos/luma_art.

2

NARRATIVES

That's My Story;
Am I Sticking With It?

"My dad always describes himself as 100% Italian. When I called him and told him that my DNA results say 19% Italian, he hung up the phone."

For Jenna's dad and others like him, their ethnicity based on their Italian culture is defining and nonnegotiable. I cannot tell you how often a person in a college class or business training begins a sentence with, "Well, first, let me say that I'm Italian," as if everything after that will make sense only in this context. One student whose results indicated about 75% Italian ancestry responded, "What a relief. My family is so Italian. We have huge dinners every Sunday, I have about a zillion cousins, and I have never eaten in a chain Italian restaurant." Of course, this kind of group identification is not limited to people of Italian heritage. Indeed, most families have **defining narratives** about their ethnic ancestry and stories about how their relatives came to America or were the first Americans. They provide evidence from old photographs and family stories. More accomplished genealogy buffs share proof that may include newspaper clippings, Census records, and, today, DNA profiles.

When new DNA results do not fit our **known narrative**, and that known narrative is central to our identity, what happens? Do we question the DNA results? Do we adjust our narrative? Do we modify the way we construct that same identity? Let's explore the construction of identity through narrative and consider why direct-to-consumer DNA testing may or may not change how a person identifies, despite a DNA profile that can challenge a known background.

Walter Fisher's narrative theory[1] and his exploration of what establishes "narrative proof" is helpful in understanding how direct-to-consumer DNA results could impact how one identifies. But first we draw on some of the literature on family narrative to help explain the importance of social identity and the role it plays.

How Do Family Narratives Shape Identity?

Life is complex and narrative stories help us capture complex experiences in thumbnail. Describe your favorite movie in 10 sentences or less. What do you include? What is forgotten or ignored? Why did you make these choices?

As experiences are translated into words, they are organized in ways that can easily be recounted in everyday conversation.[2] They are recounted in ways that resonate with the storyteller and the listener in some way. Significant stories are told and retold time and time again. Think about a recurring family event (Thanksgiving dinner, weddings, funerals, etc.), and the stories that come up at every occasion. "Your great-great-grandfather came to this country without a penny." "The first thing your father said when you were born was, 'He has the Seligman's hairline.'"

Family therapist and scholar Elizabeth Stone tells us that our family narratives are shaped over time to neatly maintain a sense of coherence, identity, and esteem. These stories are not random; rather they "give messages and instructions ... offer blueprints and ideals ... issue warnings and prohibitions."[3] They carry the family's identity, hopes, and dreams. And they are real for us. Have you ever heard someone say that some family quality (volunteerism, travel, loving chocolate) is "in our DNA"? And like DNA, family narratives cross generations. Stone explains that family narratives feel like they are in our "blood coursing down undiluted and unalloyed"

---

1   Fisher, 1985, 1989.
2   Martin et al., 1988; Zeitlin et al., 1982.
3   Stone, 2017, p. 5.

TABLE 2.1 Ethnicity estimate for Jenna

Europe East	47%
Poland, Slovakia, Hungary, & Romania	
Europe South	19%
Southern Italy	
Europe West	19%
Middle East*	5%
European Jewish*	4%
Liberian Peninsula*	4%
Ireland/Scotland/Wales*	1%
Africa North*	< 1%

*low confidence rating

and "pushing through our skin."[4] It is no wonder that we are hesitant to give them up.

At the opening of this chapter, we heard about Jenna, whose father was upset because her ancestry profile revealed only 19% Italian heritage (see Table 2.1). Upon closer discussion, Jenna shared that her mother does not identify as genetically Italian. Also, Jenna's dad really knows nothing about how his more distant ancestors came to southern Italy. Looking at Jenna's profile, we see that Jenna's ancestors were spread across Europe, Northern Africa, and the Middle East, with Italy smack in the center. But that story would be very complicated to share when people are introducing themselves at a party or bantering over a casual meal. Also, for Jenna's dad, being Italian carries a kind or clarity, acceptance, and pride that Jenna and her family have enjoyed. They like that this identification helps them fit in. They enjoy their robust Italian identity, the food, the holidays, the culture, 100%. Therefore, it is easy to see how other aspects would recede and may be greeted with surprise and rejection.

---

4   Ibid., p. 4.

Our original research from the DNA Discussion Project, which we will be referencing throughout the book, confirms this pattern. When people find unexpected ancestry in their backgrounds, 31% of those who identify as White and 22% who identify as non-White say that they intend to do "nothing" about it, no further research, no family discussion, no change in narrative, nothing.

This finding was initially one of the most surprising for us. Consider the reaction of one project participant, a graduate student studying in the sciences, after she took the test. She is from Iraq and her family had discouraged her from taking the test. "We know our heritage; what are you trying to start?" is how she summarized it. She shared the narrative of her family and was able to list her "full" name, including many, many surnames reflecting her bloodline going back generations. She shared things that surprised her in American culture, first among them the practice of adoption and giving a child the last name of the adoptive family. She admired the practice but added that she could not imagine it because "knowing your bloodline is essential." This woman thought of herself as a woman of color, Middle Eastern, and linked to a north African heritage. When her DNA profile reflected a strong European influence (not surprising looking at her), she was outraged, saying "a person's identity cannot be changed, even by a DNA test." Clearly, genetics are only a part of our ethnic/racial identity. Today, we are faced with decisions about genetics informing what we already know and feel.

Let's consider why, given new ancestry information, Jenna's father, our Iraqi student, or anyone may choose to maintain their same exact narrative. Will they forever ignore the science, or will they maintain their identification and tweak their narrative to incorporate the science? Over time, might people even change how they identify? Will they change their definition of their culture and ethnicity? Would you?

Fisher's Narrative Paradigm

In a college classroom, we often talk about **rational thinking** as the highest form of reasoning. We learn about the **scientific method**. We study Aristotle's concepts of ethos, pathos, and logos and are often left concluding, as did Aristotle, that logos, logical reasoning, is to be honored above all the forms of persuasion. Attending college is a way of training us in this superior approach.

But in your own everyday life, is this true? Do you calculate the rational reasons for falling in love? For deciding what social event to attend? For making new friends? Or avoiding others? Are there narratives in your head that push and pull you in certain directions and are not subject to being scrutinized via the scientific method? According to theorist Walter Fisher, narratives are the key to a special kind of reasoning that has its own import and standards of proof.

Fisher's narrative approach is built on the belief that humans are "storytelling animals."[5] Fisher believed that there are elements of human experience and behavior that can only be understood through stories. These stories carry not only our facts but our values. They have a beginning, middle, and end. According to Fisher, for such a story to be successful, it must meet two standards of narrative proof: narrative coherence and narrative fidelity.

Coherence

Narrative coherence asks if the story holds together, if it is cohesive, if it makes logical sense. If, for example, someone tells you that her great-grandmother fled Ireland during the potato famine and she feels very spiritually close to her and she identifies as Irish and she has red hair and freckles, you are unlikely to question her story. The facts hold together, and you have heard such stories before. DNA data has revealed to us that stories that are true are not necessarily believed and stories that are not true are often accepted as fact. Without benefit of a DNA profile to corroborate or contradict this story, this particular story seems unquestionably true. In communication scholar Joann Keyton's discussion of narrative, the scholar explains that "legitimacy in this case is not located in truth. Rather, legitimacy depends on the narrative's plausibility."[6] One question today then is, do DNA tests make new stories plausible?

---

5   Fisher, 1985, 1989.
6   Keyton, 2005, p. 89.

Fidelity

In addition to narrative plausibility is narrative fidelity. Narrative fidelity asks if the story rings true. Does it square with what you know? Suppose the young woman telling you the same story about her great grandmother has dark brown skin and kinky brown hair? You are unlikely to verbally challenge the person's account, but will you negate the story internally? She's not really Irish. Over time, might this second person give up the story because it just does not fly socially? Does she have less of a right to it?

Suppose both of these young women take a direct-to-consumer DNA test and have identical percentages of Irish ancestry—16%. Will this puny amount dissuade our red-haired friend from calling herself Irish? Will it embolden our brown-skinned friend to revive her story? Now, consider that these two young women go online to explore their DNA information and find that they share relatives in common. Does that change your perceptions of them both?

In general, our DNA Discussion Project experience would suggest, maybe. At present, we have found that people seem more flexible about identity within the same racial group. For example, a person who discovers that one or more ancestors were of Scandinavian rather than Irish ancestry, as expected, may be surprised but would find the new information reasonable. Further, they and others would still accept that this person can adopt an Irish identity. Sociologists Wendy Roth and Bjorn Ivemark tell us that "it means something quite different for a White American of Scottish descent to adopt a Black" identity and conversely for a Black person to adopt a White one.[7] This is not always the case. For example, Irish participants have found British ancestry upsetting and European Jews have found German ancestry upsetting. But, overall, owning or finding an unexpected racial group is more jolting and harder to negotiate. Such may be the issue with the two "Irish" young women. Will direct-to-consumer DNA tests change both the coherence and fidelity of their narratives?

In one test round, a White student who describes his family as extremely conservative found 1% Middle Eastern in his background. Of course, 1% is quite negligible and has an error range that could include 0, but participants normally do not consider

---

7   Roth & Ivemark, 2018.

error ranges when they react to their results. He shared that a few of his family members were upset with the findings. The Middle Eastern background had no fidelity for them. In classes, bringing a world map or historical passages to explore the nature of variances is helpful. Such conversations often lead to discussions of human migration, war and conquest, and the social construction of race. That is a goal of the DNA Discussion Project. A side effect is often to change what people think is believable in a family narrative. Still, sometimes DNA profiles are totally from left field and may be the result of a family gap or secret. The ideas of coherence and fidelity become salient in these cases as well.

Further, while we may like to think of DNA science as unchangeable, as the technology improves, we find that reported DNA results change. Any result is only as good as each lab's database. Thus, DNA "stories," even from the same lab, can change over time. What happens when a person receives results, accepts or rejects them, and then finds out a year later that their results have changed? How does this influence coherence and fidelity of any family narrative?

Strategic Narratives

In editing any family narrative, narrative coherence and fidelity factors are at play. A narrative has to be both presented convincingly and accepted socially. Narratives have a mission: to give the narrator the best deal possible under the circumstances. This being the case, certain elements are sharpened, some elements are softened or altered (if the lie passes narrative muster), and other elements seem to fade into our backgrounds, are deemed not necessary, plausible, or beneficial in specific situations.

Strategic Editing

One possible example of strategic editing relates to predictions participants made about Asian ancestry in our research pre-survey. Subjects who participated in our research, when asked what they expect in their ancestry profiles, rarely predicted any Asian ancestry. In fact, in one research iteration, we did not find one person without a known Asian relative (for example, a parent or grandparent) predicting any Asian ancestry. The most common exclamation upon seeing unanticipated Asian results was, "Where did that come from?" Given how often Asian Americans are asked "Where did you *really come* from?" perhaps these non-Asian people cannot imagine that this Other is within them. People who took this stance often had no narrative explaining the ancestry, exemplifying lack of fidelity to their lives.

It is interesting to point out that attitudes about Asian ancestry have changed over past decades. Not so long ago, Japanese Americans were interned during World War II and prior to that, in the 1800s, America had Chinese exclusion laws.[8] Today, we have more positive cultural narratives about Asians. In the past, such heritage might have been disavowed. Of course, even today, some people find the "positive" stereotypes of people of Asian background restrictive and not resonant.

Consider that recently one student shared his ancestry results in a class discussion of DNA findings. Most of the students in this learning community knew each other fairly well. The student said, "Well, 20% of my profile is Asian." The class fell silent. "Yeah, my grandmother is Chinese," he said. Not one student in class knew that. I asked the student if he just thinks of himself as White, and he hesitated and said, "Well, yeah."

Another student who identifies as half-Asian half-White experienced yet another kind of nonresonance of his Asianness. Regardless of how he tried to identify, his peers insisted on seeing only his Whiteness and refused to believe he was also Asian. This happened among both White and Asian friends. The Asian American Organization on campus called him "racist" for "culturally appropriating" their race, and a White friend laughed when he found out he was biracial, saying, "You're White as salt." This raises the issue of fidelity, but from the perspective of social acceptance. How should and do individuals faced with issues of social resonance manage their identities? Should they let silence speak for them, as with the young man in the learning community, or do they constantly challenge others' ascriptions like the other student?

When ancestry is strategically (consciously or unconsciously) dropped from a narrative, outing it can feel like a confrontation. In a recent class, one student actually yelped in class when she reviewed her results. Later, in her reflection paper, she wrote, "My

---

8   Yoon & Chin, 2020.

parents have always said negative things about Asians, so it was funny to find 10% in my background." In class later she said, "I think my parents were only kidding." They may have been kidding, or could their rejection of this ancestry have been a cover for a family secret?

Some variation of these students' behavior has happened many times. Students who look White and have non-European relatives in their backgrounds begin to identify themselves as White or just "don't mention" the other parts of their backgrounds. This was once referred to despairingly as "passing," especially among African Americans. Over time, the narrative of a distant relative fades away. When questioned, these individuals often say that they are not ashamed of their non-European backgrounds; it is just that "owning" it would seem to give the "wrong impression"—they see themselves as just like their majority peers, and they don't like the narrow projections given to them when they claim non-European heritage. Stereotypes of non-Whites can range from smart with low social skills to criminal, angry, and stupid. Since their phenotypes do not give them away, they are often silent, supported by the prevailing social narrative, until a DNA test exposes them.

It is noteworthy that this pattern does happen in the opposite direction, with people who have significant European ancestry identifying as Black or Latinx, in particular. These individuals are sometimes shocked by the diversity in their backgrounds and sometimes unhappy about it, for various reasons. The minority identification, unlike "passing" as White, has often had its genesis in relegation to "purity tests," second-class status, and marginalization.

Indeed, African Americans and Latinx individuals expect that they have different races in their backgrounds. In our research, we found that people of color were far more likely than Whites to predict multiple races in their ancestry.[9] African Americans often associate the European part of their ancestry with slavery. They also predict (often incorrectly) Native American ancestry.[10] African Americans, like Whites, are generally surprised when Asian or Middle Eastern show up in their profiles. Although African Americans think of themselves as Black and, thus, of African ancestry,

---

9 Foeman et al., 2015.
10 Lawton et al., 2018.

we have tested people with very little African ancestry who identify in this way. Overall, it is segregation and oppression (and a flexibility about the racial category) that leads African Americans in particular to predict genetic diversity and to accept a range of people into the group.

When questioned about this genetic diversity, many African Americas say that they think of the term *African American* as an expression of culture and affiliation almost as much as a particular genetic profile. Old "one-drop" rules that made anyone with any African ancestry Black made the African American genetic mix complex. Many African Americans do expect that people will have had that affiliation lifelong, so a person like Rachel Dolezal, who adopted an African American identity as an adult, is seen as a fraud to many African Americans.

Latinx individuals in our sample and in another study we conducted among interracial couples tend to think in cultural terms even more so than African Americans.[11] In their genetics, they may expect a mix of Indigenous, African, Asian, and European, or any combination or single background. Their own prejudices often lead them to prefer European and non-Indigenous ancestries, but they generally accept that they have a mix. Still, they may develop narratives that minimize unwelcome elements. In our experience, a DNA profile often reveals some overlooked ancestry but one still plausible to them. Relatedly, the Pew Foundation[12] found that over time, light-skinned people who once identified as Hispanic on the U.S. Census may switch to White. Their reasons are often as previously stated above: They want to be part of the mainstream, and they feel that the White designation gives them more role flexibility. Notably, in our research on White women married to Latino men,[13] we found that, over time, the White women began to think of themselves as "honorary Latinas," especially if they were fluent in Spanish. This did not happen on the part of White women married to African American men. These White women were more likely to see themselves as allies or advocates. And they were fierce advocates. This research found that White women married to Black men were as tenacious advocates for their "biracial"

---

11 Lawton et al., 2008.
12 Kohn, 2014.
13 Lawton et al., 2008.

children as their Black fathers (often more). These findings have led us to speculate that motherhood often trumps race in how many women identify.

Mothers aside, when White individuals found unexpected African (or Native American) ancestry in their own backgrounds, in addition to asking "Where did that come from?" several asked, "Can I get a scholarship?" Apparently, they felt that the best thing about being Black is the endless scholarships available. This is a great teaching moment.

In a world that is becoming ever more diverse, Latinx individuals and African Americans may have a narrative that can be meaningful to Whites. Despite their histories of leaning into Whiteness for all of the reasons addressed, these people of color do proudly own their identification and culture, understanding that much of the basis of identity is culture, not just phenotype. This raises the question of whether people are becoming more flexible in terms of who can claim cultural associations and learn to live with a certain amount of ambiguity.

Whiteness

We have implied the importance of Whiteness in the previous section; let's now unpack what this might mean. One overarching conclusion we have reached in our work is that it is just easier to be White, and given the opportunity, that is what a lot of people go for. People who claim this identity don't see it as "privilege"; they just see it as regular, normal, and part of the mainstream. Researchers talk about the "invisibility of Whiteness," and the necessity for it to be so, "a normative essence."[14] Other authors have written about the desire for European-based "ethnics" (Italians, Irish, etc.) to enter the White "mainstream."[15] In this we see that Whiteness, as much as any other racial concept, is socially constructed. Its success is reinforced at once by its normalcy and its exclusivity. Once in the club, perhaps it behooves those who cross over to distinguish themselves from the Others. A direct-to-consumer DNA test would seem to threaten that identification.

---

14 Nakayama & Krizek, 1995.
15 Haney-López, 2006; Ignatiev, 1995.

And yet, millions of people are excited about taking them. That alone gives hope that we are open to new knowledge.

Despite the Whiteness narrative, many European (and African American) test takers have narratives in their families that they have Native American ancestry. The "proof" is often a relative with high cheek bones or a long dark braid. Few of these stories are related to the modern Native American, and often the DNA does not bear out the stories. We have wondered why so many people have narratives of Native Ancestry unsubstantiated by the DNA and have come to the belief that in addition to the romantic and mythic images society maintains of Native Americans, despite their current lived conditions, people believe that having some Native American "blood" gives them a connection and right as Americans. It is possible that their Indigenous ancestry is so far removed that they did not inherit any of it. Strangely, this respect for connection to the land does not seem to extend to some of the people who have the most Indigenous ancestry, Latinxs.

Asians and Latinxs typically do not overestimate their Native American ancestry. Asian individuals will sometimes display Native ancestry because of the overlap with the first American's path through Asia and across the Bering Strait (and possible other paths), and Latinxs often have DNA Indigenous to the Americas. The people who are often surrounded by a powerful narrative as "illegals" tend to have the most Native ancestry, yet they often experience terrible treatment from groups who do not have that ancestral connection to the land.

All of this pushes us to consider the condition of people whose phenotypes reveal non-European ancestry. Of course, many people of color are extremely proud about their ancestry, but that's not the point. The point is that as a person who is an "Other," people often project narratives onto them that limit their psychological and physical mobility, even safety, in the world. New DNA gives us the opportunity to see where we link across lines of culture and race that see all of us as multifaceted and of broader ancestry, all essentially human.

A final element of Fisher's narrative paradigm that is relevant here is his notion of the "ideal audience," the receiver and coparticipant in narrative construction. The ideal audience is one that embraces stories because they contain messages that appeal to the better values of human nature. Fisher offers a hope that we can create a more ideal audience, one seeking narratives of love, friendship, complexity, and community. The popularity of DNA may lead to what social scientists Elizabeth Hirschman and Donald Panther-Yates say could be a "transformation in the way that race and ethnicity are conceived and acted on in the popular consciousness."[16] This is clearly consequential in the discussion of human identity, as explored here. DNA tests can help us construct the notion of complexity and richness, not taking away, but adding to our identification. In many ways, we are talking about a renegotiation of race. Ronald Jackson's cultural contracts theory may be helpful here.

What Cultural Contracts Grow From Narratives?

Jackson's Cultural Contracts

Communication scholar Ronald Jackson states that "identity negotiation is about alterations in worldview,"[17] in other words, how we make agreements on how we will see the world. Our worldview includes how we see ourselves in relation to others. Hecht suggests that individual identity is always created and maintained in interactions with others.[18] Our intrapersonal negotiations and resulting decisions as to how we identify, in other words, do not occur in a vacuum, but are affected by our relationships with others. The process involves holding on to and letting go of parts of ourselves as we accept or reject others' beliefs, norms, preferences, and judgments.

Hecht, Jackson, and Pitts explain that there are three types of social contracts people take on that could impact their identities. The first is the "ready-to-sign" contract, characterized by the goal of assimilation, often exercised by members of the dominant culture who expect others to accept their worldviews. The second is the "quasi-completed" contract, which requires adaptation, met by

---

16 Hirschman & Panther-Yates, 2008, p. 64.
17 Jackson, 2002, p. 365.
18 Hecht, 1993.

some consideration of both sides. Third is the "co-created" contract, which comes as a result of a full renegotiation of the existing social contracts. Jackson states, "The tragic reality is that most people neither understand all of the contracts they have signed nor all of the implications of having signed them."[19] We don't think critically about the deals we make in society or the conditions we adjust to without thought. We can sometimes see, in a moment of DNA discovery, some of the contracts we have signed unawares.

Ready-to-Sign Contracts

Perhaps the best example of the ready-to-sign contract signed by a person's ancestors is in the case of a gentleman who participated in the DNA project identifying as 100% European. When his results came back, they were, indeed, predominantly European. However, the test revealed that 69% of his ancestry was European Jewish (see Figure 2.1). He had no idea. Given that the area in which his prominent family lived had been known for its anti-Semitism, it is not hard to imagine that the family made a conscious decision to drop that aspect from their narrative. He reported that he had never heard anyone in his family say that they had a Jewish background. Perhaps someone accepted a ready-to-sign contract.

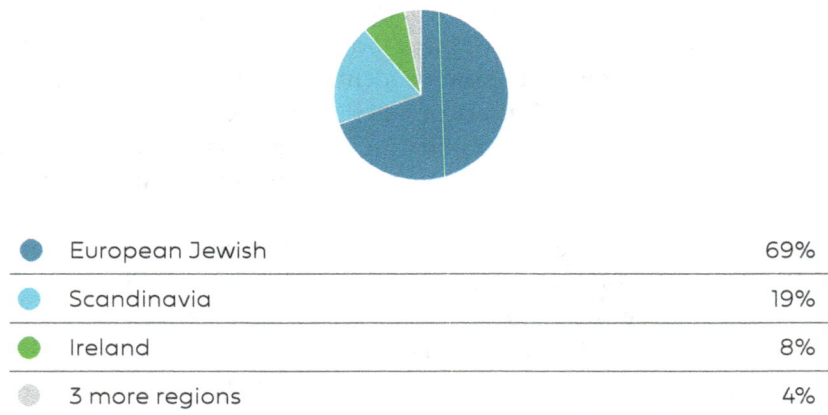

●	European Jewish	69%
●	Scandinavia	19%
●	Ireland	8%
●	3 more regions	4%

Figure 2.1 Ethnicity Estimate

---

19 Hecht et al., 2005, p. 362.

Ready-to-sign contracts are apparent in the case of immigrants, many of whom are shocked by the passion by which racial discourse occurs in the United States. Many come from places where racial categorizations do not exist the way they do in the United States and the way they handle this is by accepting the salience of race, and perhaps even accepting the hierarchy of different racial groups in American society (and their own position in the hierarchy). They react to this knowledge in different ways. For some who are light-skinned who are assumed as White, the tendency is to go along with it.[20] That is, until something offensive is said about the other part of their make-up, and they then may exert that identity, leading to a different type of social contract.

Quasi-Completed Contracts

Hecht, Jackson, and Pitts state that quasi-completed contracts are often short-term or temporary and provide as an example **code switching** (i.e. changing one's communication style to fit different environments) by those who are able to do so.[21] Quasi-completed contracts hold something back from total acquiescence or are used to assert one's self under some circumstances.

In our research, we see such compromise contracts often among people who are biracial or multiracial. (We will further discuss multiracial identity later.) The idea of a biracial person suggests that, up until now, pure racial groups existed and were discrete and distinct. With the rise in interracial unions, the thinking would go, some people are now a mix of two distinct groups, biracial. Such a statement reinforces traditional views of race but acknowledges that groups currently mix and that race is no longer seen as so dividing. Of course, this is misleading because groups (all of whom are genetically from the same place) have always mixed,[22] especially when one more powerful group imposes itself on another. For example, "one-drop" laws existing in states like Virginia, Georgia, and others defined a person with any known African ancestry, as Black, knowing full well that many of these people had European and other heritage, some related to the very

---

20 Lawton & Foeman, 2017.
21 Hecht et al., 2005.
22 McCoskey, 2012.

slave owners who disqualified them from Whiteness. So when we test a person who says that she is "biracial, Black-White" the person often has considerably more than half European ancestry. Thus, this type of quasi-completed contract maintains the imaginary status quo while allowing some people to defy it.

DNA test results have allowed individuals to adopt quasi-completed contracts in their identity negotiations with others. We have seen this manifested in three specific ways. First, people have used DNA profiles to strategically question the status quo; that is, they feel permission to speak up when people ascribe a race or ethnicity to them that they are not. For example, "I am Guatemalan, not Mexican, see!"

A second instance of this is when someone has tried to make others feel comfortable with them by adjusting their racial identity (basically a ready-to-sign contract). However, we have heard from some Asian (and other) students, for example, whose families are immigrants who practice their culture at home (e.g., eat their native food, do their cultural rituals, etc.) but who adjust to a White majority in public. By this we mean that they carry themselves socially, as one person describes as "honorary Whites," something that Blacks are often not able to do. These Asian immigrants (and sometimes African, Latinx, and other immigrants as well) do not feel the grievances or baggage resulting from the history of African Americans in this country, and therefore initially choose to take a ready-to-sign contract and identify with Whiteness. They maintain a cultural identity in private, and when the DNA test results come in, the door is opened for them to assert their identity more fully. Finally, we have seen people who initially identify as White/European but use DNA results that would allow them to reap some benefit (like access to minority incentives) by accepting an identity that includes other races, like Native American, Latinx, or African American.

Co-Created Contracts

Co-created contracts represent openness and acceptance of other worldviews on all sides. They assume equal importance of all parties involved. It is hard to find examples of true co-created contracts, especially on a cultural scale. Existing power dynamics work against truly redefining the world, and concerns for things like racial appropriation taint some attempts for true synergy and sharing across racial lines.

One way that this type of contract is manifested is in individuals who choose to call themselves "multiracial," not half of one and half of another, but who prefer the use of the term *multiracial*. In this they attempt to show that they value all parts of their identity and prefer not to be made to choose one or the other or designate percentages. Infusing new perspectives and voices helps us to reboot old assumptions about race and allows societies to renegotiate old contracts. Young people, in particular, are good at challenging norms. Their fresh eyes and access to new communication channels, as well as more exposure to multicultural programs, bring a unique perspective to old dynamics of race. In their book, *Creating a New Racial Order: How Immigration, Multiracialism, Genomics, and the Young Can Remake Race in America*, political scientists Jennifer Hochschild, Traci Burch, and Vesla Weaver[23] argue that these factors open a door for new ways of thinking. The impact is much more profound than the superficial belief that the election of the first African American president (as important as it was) ushered in a post-racial era, the social reaction to which clearly demonstrated that such an assumption was false. Real change is broadly felt, sustained, and structural. It can be occurring during periods of great social conflict as systems struggle to shift. In our own research, we found two relevant patterns related to DNA that are helping renegotiate racial cultural contracts.

The first indication that racial contracts may be changing is that even when people say that they will not change their own identities, they say that they will add new DNA findings to their narratives. They tell friends and family. They post on social media. Often attitudes follow action. Thus, the retelling of the ancestry story changes the narrative for the individual, and even more so for the new generations that will be retelling the stories with the expanded narrative. Second, today's youth are already more flexible about racial identity, and their willingness to share data on social media spreads new narratives quickly. This generation seems poised to create a new contract with the established society.

---

23 Hochschild et al., 2012.

All in all, while direct-to-consumer DNA cannot change the human heart, new information weakens unidimensional narratives of race and offers options for broader racial identity. Knowing that narratives help us state who we are and that we are in a constant state of negotiation gives the power to control our own sense of self. This perspective gives us a new way to construct our responses to resonate with various audiences. Finally, let's take a look at the basis of this opportunity, the mapping of the human genome.

How Does New Ancestry Data Change Things?

On Monday, June 26, 2000, President Bill Clinton spoke to a gathering brought together to "celebrate the completion of the first survey of the entire human genome." At that celebration he declared "one of the great truths to emerge from this triumphant expedition inside the human genome is that in genetic terms, all human beings, regardless of race, are more than 99.9 percent the same." He goes on to say, "What that means is that modern science has confirmed what we first learned from ancient fates. The most important fact of life on this Earth is our common humanity."[24] We share the same human path.

Even leading up to that ultimate accomplishment, scientists like Bryan Sykes had begun to explore the ability to use knowledge of gene mutations and selection to track human migration. He was among the first to predict the possibility of tracking ancestry. In testing his hypothesis he sought to trace a modern human back to the 5,000-year-old iceman, one of the oldest human specimens known. Upon finding such a living person and confirming his theory he writes,

> One of the strangest, and at first, surprising things about this story ... is that Marie began to feel something for the Iceman. She had seen pictures of him being shunted around from glacier to post-mortem room, poked and prodded, opened up, bits cut off. To her, he was no

---

24 Clinton, 2000.

longer just the anonymous curiosity whose picture had appeared in the papers and on television. She had started to think of him as a real person and as a relative—which is exactly what he was.[25]

This insight is a profound acknowledgment that knowing that we are all connected can change how we see and treat one another. This connection was not always assumed. For a period of time two main theories emerged to explain the human archaeological and fossil record; one, known as the multi-regional hypothesis, suggested that a species of human ancestor dispersed throughout the globe, and modern humans evolved from this predecessor in several different locations. The other, out-of-Africa theory, held that modern humans evolved in Africa for many thousands of years before they spread throughout the rest of the world. [26] This second narrative is the one upheld in the Human Genome Project (see Figure 2.2). It is the one that traces us all back to a common genetic "Eve," mother to us all. We can trace the paths of our ancestors from one common genesis across the globe. All of this work is based on that 0.1% of human variation.

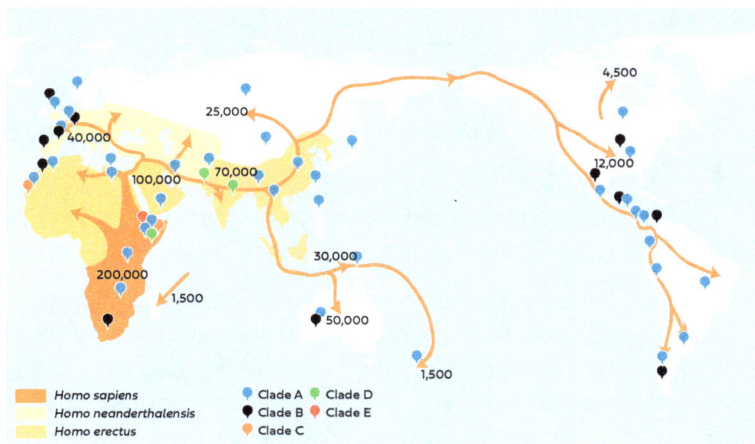

Figure 2.2 Map of *homo sapiens, homo neanderthalensis* and *homo erectus.*

25 Sykes, 2002, p. 2.
26 Gugliotta, 2008.

Clearly, people have been mixing and remixing since the beginning of human time. Even genetic tests have trouble unknotting those intersections. So much for being 100% anything. Most of the quality tests are quite good at identifying genetic relatives, so both broad and specific links seem to be the best data.

Ultimately the challenge of every individual is to determine which of the myriad factors possible will define our identity. What are the narratives that help us express our connections, our individuality, and our humanity? What will we believe about one another? As we move forward in changing a world, what is our role in shaping it as an extension of the self? In other words, what's our story?

DISCUSSION QUESTIONS

1. Do you believe that there are gaps in your family narrative? How do you think about those gaps?

2. Would any DNA finding change how you articulate your identity?

3. Has your race ever been mistaken? How did that feel? How privileged is that identity compared to the current one?

4. What would you like to preserve about the past? What would you like to change?

5. What attitudes about race that we hold today do you believe will seem obsolete 50 years from now?

6. Think of a story you often hear about some group other than your own. What was the moral of the story? Did the story make you more fearful of that group? What daily experiences have you had with people of other groups? At your place of worship? Your school? Your home?

7. Do you think it will be possible to identify an American profile? Is there a narrative that can capture a collective sense of Americanness?

ACTIVITIES

1. Try to recall a story that is told over and over in your family. What is the story? Who generally tells it? In what setting? What are the warnings and lessons carried in the tale?

2. Look at images of people online. How often do images of race seem stereotypical? How often are they ambiguous? Look at some websites that you are unlikely to view typically. Is there a difference in how race is presented?

3. Look in the mirror at your face. What untrue narrative might you construct around the way that you look? What difference would the narrative make in your life?

LEARN MORE

The Human Genome: Who Do We Think We Are?

Web Link: https://tinyurl.com/yy5qd24t

CREDITS

Fig. 2.1: Copyright © by Ancestry.com.

Fig. 2.2: Copyright © by Muhammad Ashfaq, Sean Prosser, Saima Nasir, Mariyam Masood, Sujeevan Ratnasingham, and Paul D. N. Hebert (cc by 4.0) at https://www.nature.com/articles/srep14188#Ack1.

3

AN IMMIGRANT'S PLACE

Where Are You *Really* From?

In Chapter 2 we referenced the importance of immigrants (along with the young) in changing traditional American attitudes about race. In this chapter we probe this idea by considering the immigrant story in the United States in some detail. We then explore how new DNA information blends with that story. Let us begin by talking about an immigrant's faith in coming to America.

What Is the Immigrant Story?

Every immigrant's story is a story of faith. This is true whether one leaves to flee desperate and violent conditions for the promise of safety or simply to pursue a job or education. For many, this faith is upheld; for others, the faith is rocked by realities beyond their control, one of which is how race is perceived in this country and the life-and-death consequences for individuals from particular origins. In my (Bessie's) case, my faith revolved around the doctorate I was striving for, that it would lead to opportunities for success and a better life. I am one of the lucky ones, because I came with a scholarship and a plan. I was part of the wave of immigrants with higher professional or educational qualifications that started arriving in the 70s and 80s, many from Asia.

The experience of this particular group of Asian immigrants is often invisible or fraught. It is rarely unpacked in its unique and complex elements. Many of these recent Asian immigrants were considered the "good" immigrants, with credentials and skills that would enhance the country's economic development [1] and who were advantaged by immigration policies starting in the 1960s that gave preference to skilled professionals. For us, the immigration path was arguably easier compared to others. There were difficult times, of course. While I did not lack for basic necessities and did not have fears about my legal status, I remember the aching loneliness that plagued all of us, especially my classmates from Asia, culminating in a suicide by a South Korean classmate as the weather turned colder and the days got shorter at the end of our first semester. International phone calls were expensive, most of our friends and families did not have e-mail, and there was no social media to help us keep in touch with everyone back home. I saved what I could from my stipend to buy a ticket to fly home for Christmas. For some reason, I found it really difficult to make friends with my peers who were non-Asian, and it was only years after, when I learned more about race relations and cultural styles in the United States, that I understood why this was happening.

In 2017, there were about 45 million immigrants in the United States, about 14% of the population. [2] Excluding the Natives who originally immigrated to this land about 15,000–20,000 years ago,[3] everyone in the United States is a product of immigration. The influx of immigrants from different parts of the world since the 1600s has led to a constantly changing social landscape in the United States. Immigrants have to grapple with their identity in an unfamiliar country where race is hotly contested, while residents have to adjust to their presence and the new cultures they bring in. Each new wave scuffles to fit in.

This chapter looks at how immigration changes us all. We present a short history of the nature of immigration in the United States and discuss some of the factors that could influence immigrant identification, looking at how increasingly available DNA information could play a role in the process.

---

1   Hsu, 2017.
2   Radford & Noe-Bustamente, 2019.
3   Rutherford & Mukherjee, 2017.

How Do Immigrants Adjust to the Role of Race in the United States?

I came to the United States as a PhD student in 1990 and have now spent more than half my life in this country. As with many adult immigrants, I often felt that I lived between worlds. I still constantly negotiate the pull of the Chinese and Filipino parts of my identity with the part of me that has become American. One of the social realities that struck me the most when I first arrived was how little I understood race in the United States and how this would suddenly dominate much of how I lived my life here. I have actually always had to negotiate cultures. In college, I remember writing an essay about how I had to straddle being Filipino and Chinese, two cultures that have vastly different ethnic saliences and approaches to identification.

The dominant theme of Chinese racial discourse is racial purity. Chinese culture is full of references to the "Yellow Emperor" of the Middle Kingdom who is supposedly the father of the Han race, whom all Chinese descended from. [4] The Middle Kingdom is touted as the center of the world around which others revolve, the home of the oldest civilization. Many believed one does not become Chinese except through biological descent, [5] and therefore it was imperative that one married within one's own race to preserve that purity. Racial hierarchy in China placed the Yellow Race and the "White" race as equals, dominating over the "darker" races, who were considered "feeble and stupid."[6] This belief was propagated widely in the late 19th century with even the founding father of the Republic of China Sun Yat Sen, saying,

> China was founded 5,000 years ago,
> Therefore the Yellow Emperor's name has been known since ancient times,
> He invented the compass-cart and suppressed the challenge of Chi-You,

---

4   Chow, 1997.
5   Dikotter, 1997.
6   Ibid.

Among the civilizations of the world, ours alone is the first.[7]

Filipino identification, in contrast, is characterized by fluidity and hybridity. Jordan explains that since the country has been colonized several times by different colonizers, many Filipinos are actually a mix of different races, with a variety of skin colors that range from pale to dark brown.[8] Because of American colonization, Filipinos are also fluent in English, and so they generally assimilate faster than other ethnicities when they immigrate to the United States.[9] As a result, they are often considered the "forgotten Asian Americans" and are one of the least studied minority groups in the United States.[10] Sociologist Anthony C. Ocampo laments how he was excluded from a study on Asian Americans because he was Filipino, and therefore did not meet the genetic requirements that Chinese, Koreans, and Japanese fulfilled.[11]

So I did have some experience having to think through who I was and why I make specific choices in how I identify. In the Philippines, racial hierarchy does exist, but the social hierarchy is characterized more by class. It is also a country that has high power distance (unlike the United States), which means that people generally accept power differentials among groups and therefore are more likely to accept their position in society.[12] In general, those who are lighter-skinned are regarded more highly, including individuals of pure or mixed Spanish and American descent. At the lowest level are the natives, who generally have darker skin. This bias based on phenotype continues to exist among Filipinos who have immigrated to the United States.[13] Historically, there was a strong anti-Chinese sentiment in the Philippines, but this has been toned down over time. Moreover, the Chinese community tended to stay within its boundaries when I was growing up, and I went all the way through high school with girls from Chinese families, so I never had to negotiate being Filipino versus being Chinese until I

---

7   Sautman, 1997, p. 79.
8   Jordan, 2016.
9   Osalbo, 2011.
10 Cordova, 1983; Osalbo, 2011.
11 Ocampo, 2016.
12 Hofstede Insights, 2019.
13 Kiang & Takeuchi, 2009.

went to college, although we, as other Chinese families, employed Indigenous people as servants. I was proud of my Chinese heritage, but the political environment under the Marcos Administration forced me to examine my identity and instilled a strong sense of Filipino nationalism that began to conflict with my identity as being simply Chinese. Ultimately, I chose to use the hyphenated term Filipino-Chinese or Chinese-Filipino, depending on the social circle I was with or the prevalent issue involved. No one really asked me how I identified and no one questioned my choice.

When I came to the United States as a graduate student, I had to grapple with who I was in this society. Three major themes immediately stood out, which are probably pretty common for other immigrants: the intensity of racial conflict here and the resulting need to figure out where one's race/ethnicity fell in the hierarchy, the loss of choice most immigrants really have in the identification process, and the feeling that you are always the Other.

The Intensity of Race in the United States

When immigrants arrive in the United States, they learn pretty quickly that there is a racial hierarchy characterized by severe conflict that they are pulled into and they then have to determine how their own group falls in the stratification. One of our DNA Discussion Project participants from Mexico, says, "We did not really talk about race in Mexico as much as we do here." Social identity theory[14] explains how individuals develop their self-image based on their membership in an in-group compared to out-groups, and how these interactions lead to consequences such as psychological health and life choices such as friendships, schools, where one lives, what language one speaks, and so on. In other words, the two processes involved in social identification—**self-categorization** and **social comparison**[15]—determine much of how people live their lives in relation to others. One immediately notices the diversity of racial and ethnic groups from all over the world, especially in the enclaves where most immigrants have tended to cluster, such as California and New York.

---

14 Taifel & Turner, 2004.
15 Stets & Burke, 2000.

Over the years, attitudes toward immigrants in the United States have switched back and forth between welcomed and undesired. Stereotypes have also been ascribed to specific groups. These affect immigrants' self-categorizations and give them a framework on how to compare themselves with other groups in this particular society.

Social psychologist Kay Deaux states that immigration was mostly unrestricted before 1875.[16] The countries where immigrants predominantly come from have changed over the years, leading to greater diversity in the population. After Indigenous peoples came to this land thousands of years ago, the next large wave of immigrants came from Europe in the 1600s. In 1790, Congress passed the Naturalization Act of 1790, the first law on who should be granted citizenship, identified as "free white persons of good character."[17] Slaves were brought in against their will from Africa, which would mark the beginning of a painful history between Blacks and Whites that is the major defining feature of current racial discourse in the United States. The first legal limitation enacted as a backlash toward the racially "inferior Chinaman" was the Chinese Exclusion Act of 1882, which aimed to limit Chinese laborers who had started coming in the mid-1850s to work in mines, railroad construction, and agriculture, and were viewed negatively because of the competition they posed to White workers. In the 1920s, quotas were set for nationalities, favoring immigrants from European countries, and completely excluding people from Asia, except for the Philippines, which was an American colony at that time. In 1965, the Immigration and Nationality Act ended nation-based quotas. "Skilled" immigrants and those who sought family reunification characterized the period following this act.[18] Immigrants started coming from Asia, Africa, Mexico, the Caribbean, and Central America. Many recent immigrants from Africa after this period share as much with other immigrants as they do with U.S.-born African Americans. However, they often get lumped together with the latter as if their experience was identical. Illegal immigration became a hot-button issue after 9/11, especially targeting Muslims and those coming through the Mexican border from not only Mexico but also Central American countries such

---

16 Deaux, 2006.
17 History.com Editors, 2019.
18 Ibid.

as Guatemala, Honduras, and El Salvador. The number of illegal immigrants peaked in 2007 at 12.2 million (4% of the population) and was at 10.7 million (3.2%) in 2017.[19]

The Loss of Choice

Deaux documents how attitudes toward immigration have shifted through the years. In the early 20th century, there was strong anti-immigrant sentiment that extended into the 1930s and 1940s following the economic depression.[20] With the passage of the 1965 immigration act, attitudes turned more positive, but the trend for the latter part of the century into the 2000s has been toward negative attitudes regarding immigration overall. She attributes this to three beliefs: (a) Immigrants pose a competitive threat to residents' economic livelihood, (b) immigrants pose value threats to one's quality of life, and (c) there is a hierarchy of color. The first belief persists in spite of data showing that immigration has had an overall positive impact on long-run economic growth in the United States[21] and the fact that the declining U.S. birth rate at 1.8 per woman in 2017[22] is leading to a shrinking workforce that will not be able to sustain the economy over time. The second belief arises from a fear of difference. Social scientists Marcus, Steele, and Steele describe how the "pervasive downward constitution"[23] of minorities by the **dominant White culture** has led to a decrease in tolerance and acceptance of diversity. The resulting color hierarchy is such that Whites are accorded the highest status, Blacks and Latinxs are ranked at the bottom, and Asians typically fall in between. Thus, for the contemporary immigrant to the United States, a majority of whom are either from Asia or from Latin America, entry can mean an almost automatic positioning on the color hierarchy, some distance below the dominant White. Blacks saw Asians and Hispanics, both of whom typically rank higher, as their competitors. Hispanics saw Asians as their primary threat, but not Blacks, who are typically lower.[24]

---

19 Krogstad et al., 2019.
20 Deaux, 2006.
21 National Academies of Sciences, Engineering, and Medicine, 2017.
22 World Bank. 2019.
23 Marcus, Steele, & Steele, 2000.
24 Deaux, 2006, p. 56.

In addition, when Arabs were included in the ratings, they were rated slightly higher than Blacks and Latinos, but markedly lower than Asians.[25]

Concomitant with this hierarchy are **stereotypes** about legal versus illegal immigrants in general and about specific groups in particular, often leading to both conscious and unconscious **attitudinal bias** and **behavioral discrimination**. For example, the belief that legal immigrants are more hardworking than those who are illegal has fueled anti-immigrant attitudes as the number of illegal immigrants increased in the last few decades. Since immigrants from Mexico and Central America make up the majority of illegal immigrants in the country,[26] they tend to be viewed more negatively than other groups, are viewed as not bringing needed skills to the country, and as economic liabilities.[27] In contrast, South Asian and Southeast Asian immigrants such as Indians, Chinese, Japanese, and Koreans are viewed as "good" immigrants who share the Protestant work ethic and have become stereotyped as the **"model minority,"**[28] which masks not only the high poverty rate among Asians overall and income disparities among Asian groups, but also leads to intense stress and psychological damage among many Asian students and their parents, as well as the resentment of other more stigmatized groups. This stereotype also leads many Asians to be invisible, because they are doing the right thing, are successful and do not need any help, and therefore are expected to remain silent and not rock the boat. The other face of this high work ethic image is the perception that Asians are competent but lack warmth.[29] In a legal case that started in 2014 and is still ongoing in 2020, Students for Fair Admissions sued Harvard University, claiming that the institution discriminated against Asian Americans in their admissions process. Specifically, the suit alleges that admissions officers rated Asians they had not met more negatively than other groups on "personal" ratings such as likability, courage, and kindness, in contrast to alumni interviews that showed no personality rating discrepancies.[30]

---

25 Ibid., p. 216.
26 Rosenblum & Ruiz Soto, 2015.
27 Mizrahi, 2005.
28 Suzuki, 2002.
29 Fiske, 2012; Lin et al., 2005.
30 Wong, 2018.

Political researchers Jack Citrin and David Sears[31] posit a Black exceptionalism hypothesis that argues there is a color line for African Americans (whose ancestors were involuntarily brought to the United States and suffered Jim Crow laws and extensive institutional discrimination) that is more rigid and impermeable compared to other immigrants. This critical difference in the African American experience is an important distinction because it deviates from the usual trajectory of voluntary early European immigrants and recent immigrants from other parts of the world, who generally tend to assimilate more easily.[32] African Americans continue to experience higher levels of racial intolerance, negative stereotypes, and lower levels of social integration into mainstream society, even compared to immigrants who have been here for shorter periods of time. Immigrants who identify as Black but whose narratives do not include slavery in the United States (such as those coming from Jamaica and recent immigrants from African countries) are often grouped together by other people with African Americans whose ancestors were slaves, and they have to negotiate their identity in the face of these stigmatizing stereotypes, with many choosing to distinguish their Black identity as separate, while simultaneously desiring to take advantage of opportunities created to redress damages from slavery. Native Americans are stereotyped as lazy, uneducated, aggressive, and uncivilized,[33] and people of Arab or Middle Eastern descent are often perceived as terrorists or buffoons.[34]

To be sure, narratives of race are in transition. There is higher racial tolerance among younger generations who have grown up in a society that is increasingly diverse and multiracial, and who have increasing levels of global awareness brought about by technology and travel. Nonetheless, this system pegs immigrants into value-laden positions in the existing racial hierarchy, a process over which one exerts very little control, except for those who do not "fit" expected phenotypes, such as those who are multiracial (including many Latinx individuals) and able to switch back and forth, or those whose physical characteristics make it difficult for others to ascribe specific races or ethnicities to them. One of our

---

31 Citrin & Sears, 2014.
32 Deaux, 2006.
33 Kopacz & Lawton, 2011, 2013.
34 Gerbner, 1995.

Figure 3.1 Ralph Lawton

Figure 3.2 Gaea Lawton

participants who came from Mexico laments this lack of control: "I didn't have the ethnic markers that people expected Mexicans to have and it was a huge clash between me always thinking of myself as Mexican and all of a sudden people did not believe this because I looked White." This idea that others can question or refuse to accept one's subjective identification choices is a novel experience for many immigrants who did not have to deal with this in their home countries.

Feeling That You Are Always the Other

People who are not immediately identifiable, especially those who do not look White, often face the question "Where are you *really* from?" in many of their interactions, a constant underscoring that they are perpetually considered the "Other." Another specific manifestation of this "Otherness" is the *cross-race effect,* the idea that people tend to be able to recognize the faces of the race they are most familiar with. While this type of intergroup bias occurs in all groups and has been shown to be present even among babies as young as 3 months,[35] it can be quite a shocking experience for immigrants who suddenly feel the loss of their individual identity in such a concrete manner. In graduate school, I hung out with a couple of women from Thailand and Taiwan, and classmates often mistook us for each other and used our names interchangeably

---

35 Bar-Haim et al., 2006.

because we all "looked alike" to them. This sense of Otherness persisted after I graduated, such that after I received my green card through work, I waited 10 years until my green card was set to expire before I applied for citizenship and became an American. The impetus for this was motherhood. However, like many more recent immigrants,[36] one might say I began to embrace this Otherness by choosing to keep my ethnic identifications intact. My children are biracial. I had to make a decision as to which immigrant community I would affiliate with, Filipino or Chinese, and undertook an internal cost-benefit analysis as to which would be more beneficial for my children given how each group is perceived in this society. I learned that people with mixed heritage often enjoyed the flexibility of identity choice, but still had the reality of ascription, with people usually focusing on what they perceive as the nondominant ethnicity or being denied what they felt was their identity. Thus, my son was called "Chinky Chinky" when he was a 3-year-old swimming at a pool in South Carolina, and yet he was questioned regarding his Asianness when he wanted to join an Asian club in school (see Figure 3.1).

Similarly, my daughter is often classified as "ethnically ambiguous" and is often mistaken as Latina (see Figure 3.2).

This is a common theme on Subtle Asian Traits, a popular Facebook page with more than a million members that focuses on experiences of Asians, especially children of migrants. One post states, "Sending love to other mixed race Asians who have or who are currently experiencing an identity crisis. I am ... too Asian for the White kids, too White for the Asians."

For many immigrants, therefore, choosing an identity in the United States is first a process of learning how racial conflict evolved and why it is such a dominant part of this society and then finding out where one's race/ethnicity belongs among the multitude existing here, the stereotypes and attitudes toward them, and navigating how much one wants to assimilate to a national identity versus how much one wants to keep ethnic identities intact.

---

36 Deaux, 2006.

How Does New Direct-to-Consumer DNA Play Into the Mix?

When immigrants pursue the path of getting a **green card** and citizenship, one of the documents we study is the Declaration of Independence, with its values of life, liberty, and the pursuit of happiness. We learn of other values such as equality, diversity, and the importance of a strong work ethic. And yet, it becomes quite obvious that some of this rhetoric does not quite match the realities of race, as explained earlier in this chapter. Immigrants make choices regarding their identification within this social reality by negotiating a variety of factors, such as family narratives, social networks, media portrayals, their psychological conditions, place of residence, generation, gender, religion, age, among others. With the increasing availability of direct-to-consumer DNA testing kits to determine one's ancestry, another piece of information becomes available to help them navigate this choice. Social identity is fluid. Some[37] make the case that identity is shaped and affirmed through feelings of belonging within racial and ethnic communities. Direct-to-consumer DNA testing could lead to two opposite influences on perceptions of divisions between racial and ethnic groups. On one hand, constantly updated results from companies that do direct-to-consumer DNA tests prompt us to question the rigidity and definitiveness of racial and ethnic categories. On the other hand, researchers have pointed out that direct-to-consumer DNA testing can reify beliefs of racial and ethnic differences as biological realities and can be misused to suggest biological essentialism.[38] Tajfel and Turner[39] state that individuals generally strive for a positive social identity, and through the iterative processes of self-categorization and social comparison could then move across groups or work to improve their group's perceived status. This is consistent with the idea presented in Chapter 2 that people develop family narratives strategically. In this section, we discuss some of the ways direct-to-consumer DNA information might play a role in immigrants' social identification choices.

---

37 Cross et al., 2017.
38 Phelan et al., 2014.
39 Taifel & Turner, 2004.

Social psychologists Ashmore, Deaux, and McLaughlin-Volpe[40] present a useful framework for analyzing this. They break out collective identity into (a) social categorization, (b) importance, (c) evaluation, (d) attachment and sense of interdependence, (e) social embeddedness, (f) behavioral involvement, and (g) content and meaning.

For this discussion, we take a longer-term view of who is an immigrant and draw from participants' narratives on how their families came to the United States, regardless of whether they were first generation or otherwise. We will discuss how ancestry DNA can become a part of the immigrant's collective identity using Ashmore, Deaux, and McLaughlin's framework.

Social Categorization: What Is My Group?

The first element in establishing a social identity is *social categorization*, or the act of actually placing oneself in a particular social group. This could be as simple as what name or label one chooses to call oneself. Our results show a distinct pattern in how people choose to identify before and after they take their DNA test. Immigrants from European countries tended to identify as "White or Caucasian" while a huge majority of those from other parts of the world chose their specific ethnicities instead of a more general term such as Asian.

"I am Chinese, although in America this might be Asian."

"Filipino"

"Mexican"

"Puerto Rican"

"Nigerian"

There was also a distinction among those who identified as of African descent, with those who had narratives of slavery using "African American" or "Black," and others choosing "Afro-Caribbean" or "African" or "Black African." For instance, one Kenyan

---

40 Ashmore et al., 2004.

immigrant identified as "Black African" both before and after receiving his DNA results.

Assimilation theory,[41] also called linear or straight-line assimilation theory, suggests that immigrants move through a generational process of taking on the culture of the host country, and this is predictable and strategic (toward progress and improvement). Other assimilation theories question these assumptions' applicability to non-European immigrants, stating that these other populations often maintain a strong sense of ethnicity over generations, live in ethnic enclaves, and often do not have an upward trajectory in society.[42] The image of a melting pot represents the linear assimilation model, while a tossed salad characterizes integration, an alternative view of how immigrants could keep their ethnicities intact while adopting a national identity and its social norms. Linear assimilation characterizes the process for European immigrants who came beginning the 1600s. Nevertheless, after World War II European immigrants still relied heavily on hyphenated identities (Italian American, etc.), but over time, as "White" has become synonymous with being "American," the hyphenated identities virtually disappeared.[43] Being White and speaking only English became the projected American profile. This is consistent with our findings on how DNA might affect one's choice of label. Recent immigrants are more likely to continue to mention their ethnicity first before and after they receive their test results. This is different from Whites whose families have been here for several generations, even if they are familiar with their specific ethnicities as evidenced in their narratives on how their families came over. As an example, a new immigrant who was born in Spain identifies as "Hispanic" instead of White.

Other aspects mentioned by immigrants that influenced their categorizations related to phenotype and names. For example,

"My twin brother looks mixed and has African hair."

"I would answer Lebanese because my father is 100% Lebanese and I look a lot more like him than my mother."

---

41 Gordon, 1964.
42 Portes & Zhou, 1994.
43 Citrin & Sears, 2014.

"I've always been told I had Asian facial characteristics so I thought I'd at least have some."

"Honestly I identify as Black, because I am a person of color. My skin is brown so it is easier to identify as a Black person. I believe that society will label me as a Black person also, because of the color of my skin."

Scholars[44] explain that DNA testing could be an important part of this process of self-categorization, because it gives someone the ability to claim a specific identity. However, DNA results that negated people's family names tended to be disturbing for some people. Some examples of these responses include the following:

"My father's last name is Stoudemire so I expected some German, but I did not have this in my profile."

"Because in my family we had theories for the 'Cardemil' last name, and the results destroyed my theory."

Importance: Does This Matter to Me?

The second element in establishing a social identity is *importance*, more specifically, what a particular identification is worth to one's overall self-concept. The value Chinese place on their Chinese-ness is a good example of this. Virtually all our respondents who immigrated from a Chinese country (China, Hong Kong) identified as "Chinese" before and after DNA testing. In fact, one Chinese individual who planned to participate in testing changed her mind at the last moment. When asked, she said, "I don't want to find out that I am not all Chinese." When an African American peer said, "Well, I know I have all kinds of things in my background," she responded, "Well, you know you are all mixed up; I think I am pure."

We have had similar results from recent immigrants from Nigeria and Ghana. One Ghanaian colleague almost identically carried around the DNA test kit for weeks and, in the end, never took it. When pressed, he said, "I don't want to find out I am not all Black." Yet another Nigerian participant opened her results and

---

44 Golbeck & Roth, 2012.

Figure 3.3 Ijeoma Okere

burst into tears when she found out she was not 100% Nigerian (see Figure 3.3). She questioned her test results because she was told her family descended from Nigerian royalty. And a student who goes to an HBCU (historically Black colleges and universities that primarily serve African Americans) continued to emphasize how much he and his family value their Nigerian heritage.

Evaluation: Is This Association Good or Bad?

The third element in establishing a social identity is *evaluation*, whether the individual or other people hold positive or negative associations toward the social group. On the positive end, researchers suggest that people may use genetic testing to make a claim on minority identity to gain access to **social and financial capital**,[45] such as scholarships. In terms of Native American heritage, one research team[46] identified a group of Wannabes, individuals with "minimal proof of connection" to the population who want Indigenous heritage. Among our respondents, this proof of Native American heritage was often part of a vague family narrative about an ancestor. Our results indicated a significant overprediction of Indigenous American heritage for White or Black participants, but not for other races.[47] People who had strong European ethnic identities still sometimes believed that they had Native American ancestry. One Northern European participant had such a narrative and when her profile showed no Native American heritage she offered, "Well my father lied to me about everything else, I guess he lied to me about this too?"

In terms of negative associations, interestingly, several negative attitudes among immigrants came as a result of the WWII era, and

45 Bolnick et al., 2007.
46 Goldbeck & Roth, 2012.
47 Lawton et al., 2018.

German or Jewish associations that DNA testing might show. See the following examples:

> "My father stopped speaking German, his first language, at home during WWII. He and his brother owned a farm that served as labor fields for German POWs."

> "To my mom's grandfather it was a big deal to distinguish our heritage as 'Pennsylvania Dutch' and not German. This was important to him because he wanted us to know that we came the U.S. before the war and were not part of Nazi Germany."

> "I bet the lack of family 'mythology' of our western European roots is an artifact of World War II, and the countries we didn't want to be associated with (especially Germany)."

> "My mother's side was mainly Irish but apparently one of my ancestors might have been German and they were ashamed to admit it so they pretend to be English."

> "Well ... there is some thought that previous ancestors were Jewish and arrived when being Jewish was not well received so ... we never self-identified as such."

A few respondents gave examples of aristocratic lineage or connections with famous people as a source of pride, but some were disappointed when their DNA profiles did not provide confirmation:

> "My mother did a family history dating back to the 1740's which shows us related to kings and queens of England. It was my father's side, so perhaps my DNA is more of my mother's side."

> "But I have documentation that we were related to kings and queens of England."

> "I discovered that we are descendants from Benjamin Rush, representative from Pennsylvania who signed the Declaration of Independence."

> "I've heard a story that I'm related to John Hart, who signed the Declaration of Independence."

Of course, any DNA testing should be combined with records research to confirm or disconfirm any specific historical connections. Because they had been in the United States for several generations, these respondents identified as White, although they talked about their feelings when DNA results either confirmed or did not support what they believed their ethnic heritage to be. One recent immigrant from Mexico who chose to identify as "Mexican, Hispanic, or Latino" because of negative associations with gypsies says,

> "When I was 14 years old, I was told by an aunt from my father's side that my great-grandparents (father side) came to America, and specifically to Mexico, from Hungary, and that they were gypsies. As being a gypsy was considered 'bad' and shameful, they decided to separate from their clan and live in Mexico with another last name."

Attachment and Sense of Interdependence: Do I Feel Connection to This Group?

The fourth element in establishing a social identity is *attachment and sense of interdependence*, or "emotional involvement felt with the group, or the degree to which a person feels at one with the group."[48] Regardless of whether one views a group positively or negatively, one can feel attachment to the group. One respondent was quite upset when she received her DNA results that showed no Jewish percentage, "because [her] last name is Jewish." Another respondent was adopted from China when she was 3 months old and therefore did not have experience with Chinese culture aside from having a birth certificate and a passport. She initially identified as Chinese but questioned this "because [she has] been told [she] do[es] not 'look Chinese.' [She] do[es] not have a monolid, nor is [her] hair straight and glossy. [Her] face is more angular and [she] believe[s] this is due to a mixed heritage." When DNA results confirmed her European mixed heritage, she was quite pleased. Another first-generation immigrant from Egypt expressed lack of attachment by explaining how he struggles to fit the racial

---

48 Ashmore et al., 2004.

categories used in the United States because he doesn't share the experience of specific groups. He says,

> "According to early European navigators, Egyptians are Caucasian; however, I've never completely felt 'White.' Egypt is also in Africa; however, I've never felt completely 'African American.' I identify most as Arab or Middle Eastern; however, I believe that classifies more as ethnicity than race."

Social Embeddedness: Am I Part of This Network?

The fifth element in establishing a social identity is *social embeddedness* into the group, which is a function of a person's network of social relationships. Often, respondents who do not know anyone in their families who might have come from places their DNA profiles contain would express something like what one respondent said, "No one in my family remembers anyone coming from those places; both sets of grandparents are puzzled."

Communication researchers Hecht, Jackson, and Pitts[49] discuss the anxiety immigrants feel when they come to the United States and find that they are losing their identity. This can be especially difficult for those who come alone, without a family to act as an immediate support network. When I arrived by myself, I sought out other students who also came from the Philippines and naturally gravitated to other Asian students. Similar to linguist Sharon Wilkinson's[50] findings, many international students discover that they feel a greater affinity with their national origin, and this feeling drives them to seek out people from the same country. Because of the way immigration patterns have evolved in the United States, there are now ethnic enclaves representing many cultures. In addition, one of the major impetus for immigration after the 1960s was family reunification. These ease the adjustment process for those who are able to enmesh themselves in these interpersonal networks. For example, there are many churches, community centers, and language schools serving different nationalities, allowing immigrants to continue practicing their culture.

---

49 Hecht et al., 2005.
50 Wilkinson, 1998.

Behavioral Involvement:
Do I Participate in This Culture?

These networks increase the likelihood of the sixth element in establishing a social identity: *behavioral involvement*, or the degree to which a person engages in actions that directly involve the social category. Examples of behaviors that might affect identity choice are language propagation, cultural practices such as food and religious venues, and political activities. Over and over, we heard respondents say how culture trumps biology in their process of identification.[51] Several African American students felt so strongly about this that they were often critical of other people who felt they could claim a racial identity because it was on their DNA profile. But this was true not only among those who identified as African American. Anthropologist Yulia Egorova[52] studied members of Bene-Israel Jewish ethnic group in India and found that everyone in their study rejected both the need and the authority of DNA tests in proving their ethnic identity. Similarly, respondents explained why they would stick to their identification regardless of their DNA results:

> "Black because that is the culture I was raised and the culture that I know."

> "Because I wear hijab and it seems easier I go with 'I'm Arab' and the fact that that seems to be a more adequate measure."

> "My mom was raised in a German enclave in Indiana called Darmstadt. Many of my family traditions have German roots, such as hiding a pickle on the Christmas tree for people to find and win a prize."

> "I never thought of being 5% Middle Eastern, but it does say it was the birthplace of religions like Christianity, which is my dad's side. And it includes Jewish countries, like my mom's side."

> "Chinese, I speak Cantonese fluently, which is the mostly used language in Hong Kong."

---

51 Lawton & Foeman, 2017.
52 Egorova, 2009.

Language, in particular, is a strong predictor of whether one would keep one's ethnic origin as part of their identity. On Subtle Asian Traits' Facebook page, there are countless posts on the backlash people receive when they speak in a different language:

> "So one of the guests who came by my nail spa was with one of my technicians who happens to be Taiwanese. When my technician told her I was Filipino, she goes 'So you're both Asian?! You understand each other?!' Then she proceeded to make us each speak things in our different native languages because she didn't know we all spoke differently and thought Asian was a language in itself."

One respondent lamented how her family discouraged her from speaking Italian. "My mother's family in particular all spoke Italian, but would not teach us children or speak it in front of us. They felt it was important that we assimilate into American culture." Similarly, Filipinos often speak very good English, and many discourage their children from learning Filipino so they can assimilate faster, which leads to abandonment of their culture.[53] In contrast, Chinese language schools can be found virtually everywhere Chinese immigrants gather and children are pressured to go to these schools whether they want to or not.[54]

Content and Meaning: Who Are We?

The seventh and final element in establishing a social identity is *content and meaning*, which include traits, **group consciousness**, or collective memory associated with the group. The latter includes what is called the "story of me as part of the group."[55] One respondent drew on traits when he questioned his DNA results, which did not match what he was always told—that he had a German "work ethic" and an Irish "temperament." African Americans often talk about their link to slavery. One individual talked about group consciousness of Italian and Irish heritage:

> "My whole life I have been told that I am Irish ... my family has never talked about a potential ancestor from Asia. ... Both

---

53 Osalbo, 2005.
54 Lawton & Logio, 2009.
55 Ashmore et al., 2004, p. 96.

sets of grandparents came to the U.S. around the turn of the
last century. For my mom's family my grandfather came over
alone and left my grandmother and two sons behind in Italy,
he then made enough money to get them all over to the U.S.
Three more children were born here including my mother;
however, in the 1920s, the entire family moved back to Italy
for a while. I have my grandmother's passport that includes
a picture of her and all the children. A copy of that passport
is now part of the Ellis Island collection."

Or,

"My mom is White and my dad is Puerto Rican. That is the
narrative I've always believed. But given that I am 80% European, I feel there may be more to the story. It changes my
narrative … and, wow, I'm THAT White?!"

Overall, DNA information brings the opportunity for people to
consider their own immigration story, regardless of how long they
or their family have been in the United States. It could lead one to
question the authenticity of one's family narratives, but it could also
lead to affirmations of the identity choices taken by their ancestors.
Among non-Whites, unexpected DNA often leads to adjustments
in identification. What was missing in the conversation among
most of our respondents was consideration of the intersectionality
of other factors such as gender, social class, or even age in those
identity choices. For example, how might a Chinese grandmother
who came to live with her children and grandchildren respond
differently compared to a young woman who was adopted as an
infant? Might women coming from Middle Eastern cultures that
have stringent norms and rules for women more readily embrace
new identities? DNA information opens opportunities for further
conversation on how an immigrant chooses to identify in this
racially conscious society.

DISCUSSION QUESTIONS

1. At what age do you think immigrants start thinking of them-
    selves as primarily American instead of their place of birth?

2. Think about immigrants in your family, if any. What do they give up and what do they retain from their original culture?

3. Do you think immigrants are changing how we think about race? How?

4. When you talk to immigrants, what has surprised them about the United States when they first arrived?

ACTIVITIES

1. Bring in some artifact from your family's old country's past (it can be Indigenous to the Americans) and discuss its origin and meaning.

2. Find a person online who immigrated to the United States and ask what surprised them about topics of gender, race, and so on in the United States.

LEARN MORE

DNA, Adoption and Identity—Mixed Bag: Culture, Adoption and the Transracial Family

Web Link: https://tinyurl.com/y5juor25

CREDITS
Fig. 3.1: Copyright © by Ben Shepard. Reprinted with permission.

Fig. 3.2: Copyright © by Andrew Steinman. Reprinted with permission.

CHAPTER

4

RESEARCH ABOUT IDENTITY AND DIRECT-TO-CONSUMER DNA

What Are We Learning?

In our original research on the relationship between direct-to-consumer DNA tests and identity we are learning some interesting things. When we first started to look at patterns in responses before and after people took their direct-to-consumer DNA test, we wanted to ask certain questions: How did participants react to their DNA profile? How did others react when participants told them their profile? Would they change their family narratives as a result of their DNA test? Would they change how they answer when people ask them how they identify? How about their Census identification? What other behaviors, if any, would they change?

As communication scholars, we wanted to understand the impact of genetic DNA information on identity, not just because this affects interpersonal relationships, but also because it has implications for how society functions. For example, census patterns are used to determine resource distribution, political districts, and a host of social programs. This is, therefore, not just an issue of internal negotiation, but has real-world practical repercussions.

In this section, we present some of the results we have found in our research, especially as findings relate to how people say DNA profiles will affect how they will identify on the **U.S. Census**.[1] We will discuss three principal themes that generalize some of our findings. First, we discuss how people reject the findings and

---

1   Foeman et al., 2015.

question, "Is that right?" Second, we look at how people do share and internalize their findings, some fascinated asking, "Isn't this something?" Finally, we explore how people who already identify as multiracial answer the question "Which am I?"

Is That Right?
How People Reject the Findings

First, in general, we found that participants do not change their formal Census identification based on DNA data, even if the DNA profile is quite different. This finding suggests that participants distinguish between genetics, narrative, and identity. For many participants, their identity is based on narratives that are plausible but may conflict with genetic reality. Based on their resistance to this change, participants' racial identity seems to have firmed up perhaps early in life, especially for people in the majority culture. Despite the fact that participants were intrigued and excited by unexpected results, overall they did not seem willing to integrate a new sense of racial identity as a result of the genetic data. This holds implications for communication scholars who study identity, because it underscores the power of family lore in identity formation, despite scientific information that may not support these narratives. Said one respondent who identifies as African American,

> "It feels like somehow, some way my results were mixed up and I received the wrong profile. There has never been mention of [this] heritage in our family. ... Truthfully, I wouldn't adjust my family narrative."

Participants report they will share results with friends and family, as well as include the new information as part of their "story," but few said that they would change their racial identification on the U.S. Census form. In fact, one participant, who found that her ancestry was predominantly European, although she identified as a Middle Eastern woman of color, said unequivocally that "nothing can change a person's identity, even DNA." Previously existing narrative proof seems to outweigh new genetic information.

Despite the attitude of this woman of color, overall, Whites were stronger in holding on to a single identity, were more likely to overestimate their "Whiteness," and were most resistant to changing it. It is likely that people in the dominant group consciously or subconsciously experience little benefit in switching from White to multiracial. For example, one respondent who identified as White said,

> "The findings of this DNA were extremely shocking to my mother. I do not believe I would change any parts of my family narrative because I was raised with certain traditions, and I cherish the memories of learning those traditions more than I do other aspects of my ethnic background. I will continue to identify as White."

Similarly, another respondent who identified as White said,

> "I am happy I got the DNA test, but I am not taking it seriously. My family are all immigrants from Italy and traveled here for a better life, and they have achieved it. I believe my family has not hidden anything from me and we are in fact Italian. Regardless of these results, I still consider myself to have a 100% Italian background."

We would reiterate our reference to the "one-drop" laws in Chapter 2, and articulated in a Tennessee ruling, which, in 1910, defined as Black anyone "having any African blood in their veins." This left Whites constructing White as "pure" and unadulterated. According to Hickman, "it has created the African-American race as we know it today" and has also left the illusion that those who classify themselves as "White" have no "African blood."[2] This American myth seems to reveal itself at the level of the family and personal narrative. One participant called her mother after her ancestry test results reported that she is approximately 25% African (both north and Sub-Saharan African). The mother responded to the report by saying, "That's not right and you're not ours." African Americans, on the other hand, know that their ancestry is complicated by a history of slavery and Jim Crow. Thus, African Americans may already think of themselves as multiracial and are both more flexible to change and may already see the term African American as encompassing a multiracial mix.[3] Even for other racial groupings,

---

2   Hickman, 1997, p. 1,163.
3   Ibid.

however, we found that when participants showed willingness to change their identification, this change came in the form of *adding* to their identification, as opposed to re-categorizing it. Non-Whites also tended initially to self-identify with multiple groupings (for example, African and Native American ancestry),[4] as compared to Whites. In addition, identifying as African American may also be perceived as a political statement as well as a racial one. Indeed, there have been campaigns to encourage African Americans to select "Black" as their single racial identifier on the U.S. Census for political reasons. As a result of this feeling, there may be pushback against the prospect of re-categorizing oneself as other than African American. One student grew up identifying as African American and wanted to have a DNA test completed because a relative recently told her that she has Latina background. The student, who has a dark brown complexion, had a DNA profile that was almost 50% European. She posted her profile on Facebook and then reported that she was barraged with negative feedback. One person commented very caustically on her dark skin and concluded, "What, you gonna go around and tell people you're European now?" Clearly there is pressure from outside as well as internally to stick with a story that has proved coherent up to that point.

The Latinx designation is not a racial identification in the same way that European, Asian, or African ancestries are associated with specific geographic locations and genetic lines. In fact, the U.S. Census includes two separate questions about background for people with this identification. One specifically asks about Latinx identity and a separate question asks about race, so a person can be of any race and still identify as Latinx. The association of people who identify as Latinx is complex and may actually provide a great deal of flexibility within the term, so participants may feel that no new designation is required regarding how they identify on the Census.

How does one begin to merge conflicting genetic and narrative data? Participants focused mainly on the effects that the genetic information might have on their own families' relationships and dynamics, implying that perhaps the starting point for merging narratives is situated not within individuals or among friends but at the level of family members communicating with each other.

---

4   Nelson, 2000

Several talk about sharing test results over Thanksgiving dinner. A common attitude is, "Isn't this something?"

Isn't This Something? How People Integrate the Findings

The second point we want to discuss is that participants do show willingness to share DNA information and to initiate efforts to learn more about their background, opening the possibility of shifting narratives across generations. Participants generally showed surprise or had positive attitudes toward their DNA profile. Most shared their profile with others, who were also surprised or curious about the results. About half of participants exhibited willingness to do more research and dig deeper into their background. One respondent who identified as White shared,

> "I called my mom, who was just as surprised as me by the high percentage of South Central Asian. I told my two best friends, and they did not understand how that would be possible. I ended up feeling stupid because I did not even have a good explanation for them. About 2 weeks later I went home for the weekend to visit my family. My aunt heard about my DNA results and denied that we were from that part of the world. Then she told me how our ancestors were from Germany, then settled in Siberia close to the Ural Mountains. I later found out that the Ural Mountains border Kazakhstan, which is considered a South Central Asian country. It suddenly made sense to me after I did more research."

It is possible that if participants of all backgrounds continue to share DNA information with their children, their children will grow up with a different sense of self and a broader racial identity, which has major implications for the construction of race into the future.[5] U.S. culture is already leaning toward a more multicultural self-image, with attitudes toward interracial marriage being more positive than ever[6] and the U.S. Census now offering the option of indicating more than one race. Our participants express that

5   Hirschman & Panther-Yates, 2008.
6   Wang, 2012.

DNA data may be too far ahead of a familiar story to make much real difference in their own lives. Fisher's concepts of coherence and fidelity help explain this phenomenon as well as a construction of race centuries in the making.[7] People are often locked into their family narratives because these have made sense to them; they work for them. One respondent explained how her Native American heritage has benefitted her family; thus, she did not welcome results showing she had very little Native American DNA:

> "I defined myself as being Native American. I still am, but not as much as I thought I was. I am still toying with the idea of keeping my mouth shut about the DNA test to my family. My paternal aunt "Shining Star" is deeply steeped in Native American culture. For her to find out that Poppop Ho was basically lying would break her heart. Some of us had full rides to college because we were Native American."

When DNA conflicts with these personal stories, rendering the latter incoherent or distressing, people then tend to try to make sense of the information by "doing more research" or "attending cultural events" related to their DNA profiles. When one experiences a different culture, the process of in-group belongingness and owning of this culture may begin. One respondent knew she was biracial; however, she identified as Puerto Rican and found out she was mostly European. This is what she had to say about her narrative:

> "Most of my life I grew up thinking I was just Puerto Rican, failing to admit to being European because I didn't have contact with that side of my family. I didn't have a close relationship with my biological mom, who is White. Although it is hard for me to connect with any side of myself besides Hispanic, I do love the fact that I am mixed. I do know it is something I will pass down to future generations, so they can know how diverse they are and appreciate how beautiful that is as well."

When people begin to accept diversity in their biological make-up, it then becomes more reasonable to shift a narrative.

---

7   Fisher, 1987.

For example, one of the reasons adoptive parents of children from China enroll their adopted children in Chinese language schools is to help their children feel belongingness with a community from their birthplace, helping them own this part of their identity.[8] One participant in this study of Chinese descent who had Native American ancestry in her profile was intrigued to find through further research that Asian and Native American DNA are sometimes indistinguishable because of the trek of Native Americans through Asia in the human migration. Such learning helps individuals to include new ancestry in their narratives. Perhaps the most important finding is that the presentation of new and often surprising data opens the door for a reconsideration of the common construction of race. One respondent said,

> "I would describe my DNA test as eye-opening. If this test was completely accurate, I am curious in learning more and seeking something like Ancestry.com for more information on where my family roots lie."

About one third of participants will not change any of their narrative or their behaviors even after finding out their DNA, and 75% of participants believe that society will not see them differently based on new DNA information. On the flipside, this means that two thirds of participants will initiate changes in their stories and will investigate the meaning of their genetic data, and about a quarter believe that society will change how they are viewed. As the use of these tests proliferates and people discuss the findings and develop narratives to incorporate them, we believe the broader sense of race could shift in its trajectory. As storytelling animals,[9] people will weave together a new coherent story that feeds into the social construction of race. Notice how this respondent sought to explain the finding that he was part Native American through a narrative from his mom:

> "I have always thought I was only European. My results told me I was 15% Hispanic and I have some Native American. I found out from my mom after I told her that my

8   Lawton & Logio, 2009.
9   Fisher, 1987.

great-great-grandfather was a tiny bit Native American. I
had no idea whatsoever about that until this week."

Another participant who identified as Hispanic went through
the same process of trying to find an explanation:

> "When I first received my results, I was confused by the large
> percentage of Middle Eastern in my background, but after
> the shock wore off I began to think things through in order
> to find an explanation. I looked up the origin of my father's
> name. It showed that his last name originated from Israel
> and that his family later moved to Spain. However, many
> of my friends now joke, "You're not even Hispanic; what do
> you know?" when discussing things of the Hispanic culture. I
> would have to say it has been getting annoying lately, espe-
> cially since I was born, raised, and lived in both the Dominican
> Republic and Puerto Rico. I do not let it get to me because
> at the end of the day I will never feel the need to 'prove my
> Hispanic-ness' to anyone. However, I am intrigued and have
> reached out to a close friend from Pakistan and my cousin-
> in-law from Turkey."

New awareness and a new demographic reality of the United
States surely call us to revisit the racial narrative of the United
States.[10] Strategies suggested by genetic counselors[11] can help us
process some of the challenging and perhaps disorienting information we find. Parenthetically, our work encourages people to
question DNA data and explore its nature. It therefore engages
people, especially the young and people of color, in the sciences,
encouraging them to see the biological sciences as relevant to their
lived experience. Without a doubt, the face of the United States
is changing, as is access to ancestry DNA data, and we are only at
the beginning of a new conversation about what it all means.[12]
Perhaps there is nothing more American (even more human) than
the desire to reinvent oneself, stretching the limits of possibility
to bend toward self-determination. Using communication to construct an identity in the face of new DNA data creates a fertile new

---

10 Hirschman & Panther-Yates, 2008; Lopez, 1994; Lwin, 2006.
11 Gaff & Bylund, 2010; Koerner et al., 2010; McCarthy et al., 2007.
12 Foeman, 2012; Foeman & Howard, 2014; Foeman & Lawton, 2013.

relationship between information and narrative, one that scholars of communication are in a unique position to explore. We now turn to those who are multiracial, who start out knowing they have multiple possible backgrounds in their profile. How does their genetic DNA profile affect how they negotiate and articulate their identity? They consider, "Which am I?"

Which Am I?
How Multiracial People May Lead the Way

Feeling that we do not have a clear and resonant identity group can be painful. For many people, living between groups is a constant state. In approaching this topic, we review results from the DNA Discussion Project that focused on a sample of multiracial people, specifically individuals whose parents were from different racial groups, and present a framework for looking at how respondents articulated how they identify.[13]

The term "multiracial" has been employed over the decades to explain the identity and experience of people who classify themselves as of more than one race. In the past, the term was more often imposed externally than embraced personally. Today, elements of both can be seen, and we use self-reports in our research as a reasonable strategy for assessing biracial or multiracial identification.

The U.S. Census estimates that one in five individuals will be multiracial by 2050.[14] Already shifting racial attitudes, as well as the increasing popularity of direct-to-consumer DNA testing, may further accelerate the fuzziness of race, and we explore the experiences of multiracial people to reflect the direction in which racial identification is moving.

All science—whether physical or social—involves storytelling. The process of multiracial identification involves understanding social, psychological, and **ecological** factors in each individual's story. Scholars have discussed family narratives as a kind of "willful pairing down of multiple lines of descent."[15] So, what role does

---

13 Lawton & Foeman, 2017.
14 Shih & Sanchez, 2009.
15 Wailoo, 2012, p. 14.

genetics play in this process? Each individual has genes that have been passed down from one generation to the next in a story of genetic combinations and re-combinations resulting from multiple possibilities; thus, each individual has a unique story of what was received from various ancestors.[16] Direct-to-consumer DNA interpretation is another kind of narrative, and a multitude of scientific and procedural factors shape how the DNA story is interpreted and presented. Genetic data represent thousands of years of information; family narratives and social variables are often current or go back to no more than a few generations, spanning at most a couple hundred years. In each case, the two storylines have to be reconciled in a person's mind and narratives. Ultimately, for multiracial individuals, these stories are more complex than those who believe they come from one race. Multiracial people have the potential for more fluidity in identification, resulting from the more complex social, physical, and historical contexts they have to navigate in the process.

The study of multiracial individuals has evolved dramatically over the past century, as early work[17] utilized alienating language such as "the marginal man." The title of sociologist Everett Stonequist's article "The Problem of the Marginal Man" framed the existence of multiracial individuals as a complication, implying their subordination to dominant monoracial groups in society as well as their difficulty in belonging to any of their specific races. There have been shifts in models of multiracial identification from negative to positive and from stable oriented to fluid. In addition, a number of social, psychological, and ecological factors have been identified that contribute to multiracial identity development.

Sociologist Kimberly DaCosta tells the story of how as the population of multiracial people grew, there was a push to revise the Census in the 1990s to allow these individuals to more accurately classify themselves, especially to give them the ability to honor both parents, not just one or the other.[18] This also allowed many multiracial people to express their fluidity concretely. It is crucial to point out that while there is much theory on racial fluidity among multiracial people, really only the racially ambiguous people

16   Ancestry, n.d.a.
17   Park, 1928; Stonequist, 1935.
18   DaCosta, 2007.

have this option. One dark-skinned African American in a DNA discussion session joked, "I feel that I am channeling a White man, but no one is having it." In contrast, Asians and Latinos have had higher rates of interracial marriages, and over time have been more easily able to treat race as "an optional and symbolic feature of their lives."[19] As a result, they are more easily able to assert their multiracial-ness and are experiencing what researchers are calling the phenomenon of becoming White.[20]

With the increasing availability of ancestry DNA for public consumption, we sought to explore how **genotype** information affected identification narratives of multiracial individuals by exploring patterns of articulating multiracial identity before and after taking a DNA test. Just like the Census, having access to genetic DNA information allowed individuals to grapple internally with their identification, as opposed to simply having others try to dictate this for them. In a sense, it shifts the power of decision into their hands, at least, for those who have more racially ambiguous phenotypes and therefore have the option of racial fluidity. We found four patterns that hue closely with education scholar Kristen Renn's[21] classifications, which we will discuss throughout the rest of the chapter. These four patterns of articulating racial identification by multiracial individuals include (a) the individual articulates a monoracial identity; (b) the individual articulates one identity, but that identity can shift in response to various conditions; (c) the individual articulates an "extraracial" identity, opting out of any of the traditional categories applied to race; and (d) the person distinguishes traditional categories of race from culture and owns the two identities in different ways.

Articulating a Monoracial Identity

Individuals using this pattern choose one race and stick with it. There was a different articulation of this theme across generations. Those aged 40 and older were more likely to express that they were of one race and kept this position from pre to post, regardless of DNA results. In two cases, women in their 60s, both of whom

---

19 Ibid., p. 10.
20 Zhou, 2007.
21 Renn, 2004, 2008.

identified as Black (African American), did not know until later in life that they were of multiracial lineage. One said, "I just thought my mother was light-skinned like all of the other kids I knew." She went on to say, "Before I went to college she [her mother] told me." This participant attended a historically Black college and expressed some sadness that, while there, she was not able to run for homecoming queen because it was generally accepted [during the 70s era] that she did not represent the image of Black beauty. When her DNA results reflected very little African ancestry, she sent a Facebook message to one of the authors (whom she knew personally) immediately after receipt of the results. She said, "OMG … got it!! So is this chart telling me that that little bit of that pie is all I have of African American??" She asked when results would be forwarded to another woman she knew in the study, who also discovered in adulthood that her family was not African American at all, although that was always how they identified themselves. The first woman went on to say, "OK now [she] is in shock" even though the DNA profile (with no African ancestry) confirmed what she had told the researchers. Both women continue to identify as Black. The shock they expressed upon receiving their profiles and the conflict this presented had no impact on how they continue to view themselves as singularly Black. However, the results clearly created high levels of discomfort in these two women. While they consented to write down responses to some of the post-interview questions, we were never able to complete a full face-to-face post-interview with them.

Another gentleman was somewhat younger (40s), but from the South where, he explained, he had not known any other biracial people like himself. He identified as Black, although he clearly articulated details of how he appears to others, specifically mentioning his "sharp nose" and "light skin." When his profile revealed a high percentage of European ancestry and very little African ancestry, he responded, "What are you trying to do to me? You caused a lot of trouble in my family." He, too, was reticent to provide a full post-interview but provided written responses to some of the post-interview questions, where he stated that he continues to articulate his identity as that of a Black man,

> "I benefit from White privilege everyday as a light-skinned person, but my politics are as Black as the night. For me to

say I want to be entirely Black would reflect my politics. …
Today I don't identify as mixed because people who identify
as biracial do it to appease White people. In no way will I or
my kids identify as not Black."

A fourth Black-White woman with mostly European ancestry also
said that she will continue to identify as Black because the result
"does not change racial categories in the [United States]." All these
responses suggest that these individuals were led by their times and
settings to identify as one race. Furthermore, there are historical and
political reasons Black Americans would reject any White ancestry.
For example, having African slave heritage and White heritage may
be a source of pain or anger among mixed-race Black people. Finding other genetic information for these individuals was therefore
disorienting and, to some degree, undermining. On the other hand,
the phenomenon of "passing" showed that not everyone rejected
White ancestry; some chose to embrace it to avoid the norm of being
categorized under the minority race. Social psychologists Jennifer
Richeson and Samuel Sommers discussed that association could place
individuals into categories that were not consistent with how they
looked (and perhaps their underlying genetic profile) for a variety
of reasons, and that "the historical convention" was "to categorize
individuals with mixed racial ancestry into the socially subordinate
parental race."[22] This was especially so in earlier generations and in
some geographic regions.[23] It is far less likely that young multiracial
individuals do not know they are multiracial, compared to these
older participants. Therefore, the older generation tended to fall into
this first category, but not the younger ones.

Articulating One Identity that Shifts in Response to Conditions

Many participants in this category described themselves by stating
their parents' races, such as half Black and half White, half Chinese (or Asian) and half White, half Asian (or Chinese) and half
Black, or half Latina and half Black. However, participants then
explained how they would choose one racial identity depending
on the situation. This shifting was consistent before and after

---

22 Richeson & Sommers, 2016, p. 433.
23 Chen & Hamilton, 2012; Richeson & Sommers, 2016.

genetic testing. When probed, these individuals often articulated that their identities adjust in certain settings. For example, they might feel more sensitive when issues about one of their identified groups came up in school or when issues in society were discussed. Some talked about feeling one race at one family reunion and another when with the other family. One Native American–African American–White woman said, "I identify as Native American when people bitch about immigration, and I identify as African American when people are gunned down unarmed."

Several light-skinned participants said that others often just assumed they were White, and they tended to go along with that until something was said that was offensive about the other "half," and they then exerted that identity. A few participants talked about completing college applications and checking the box for African American or Latina, even as they explained how they lived day to day in a White world. One teenager said that while his peers just assumed he was White most of the time, he felt academic pressure and pride because of his Asian background, which he clearly saw as tied to both his mother's ethnic Chinese background and her status as an immigrant. Darker-skinned people were assumed to be African American by others and had to clarify when an offensive or stereotypical statement was made about Whites or Asians.

Fisher's criteria for a successful narrative informs the dilemma for people who identified as a combination of distinct races.[24] According to Fisher, a successful narrative must meet standards of coherence and fidelity. It must be both possible and resonant. For multiracial people who do not look like what society expects, maintaining a biracial (two-race) narrative may be a challenge. When DNA data reinforce what is lived, the identity is supported; when DNA data contrast with the lived identity, maintaining a biracial narrative may be all the more difficult. In one case, a Chinese-Black participant reviewed results that indicated that he had inherited a largely African American genetic profile. He responded, "I have no doubt that my father is Chinese; I have no other narrative to tell. My family is confused. However, my [African American] mother doesn't care, and she finds it funny. I think it doesn't matter to

---

24 Fisher, 1987.

her because she's only ever viewed me as Black." This young man decided to go live in China.

Other pressures can force the individual to fight for each specific racial identity. One man in his 20s, whose father is African American and mother is Chinese, said that the one argument his parents had explicitly had about race was when he wanted to play basketball with an Asian team and his mother was pleased, but his father felt it was a waste of time. His father exerted himself and insisted that his son play with other African Americans. He prevailed, but the son, who liked linking to the Chinese part of his background, summarized, "That was a trip."

Sometimes comments made by participants seemed inconsistent unless viewed from this perspective. For example, one person said that she thought of herself as culturally White and racially biracial. Later she said that she would "never under any circumstances identify herself as White." Apparently in a passive way, this person allowed herself to be assumed to be part of the majority, and she articulated that it was because she related to the sense of not being limited or defined by race, which she experienced as coming along with being a person of color. So some of these people seemed to passively accept being assumed to be one race (Black or White or Asian) and seemed to go with that on a daily basis, although another identity could be called up depending on the situation they were in.

Articulating an Extraracial Identity

This parallels one of Renn's identification patterns, which viewed such classifications as resistance to traditional socially constructed categories of race.[25] This pattern was manifested in several ways. Some participants claimed a solely "multiracial" identity that was on par with other racial categories, meaning they chose to identify as "multiracial" instead of articulating a specific race or ethnicity. In contrast, everyone else had laundry lists of what was in their backgrounds, but they saw these categories as discrete, rather than as one multiracial whole. Four of the youngest participants expressed wanting to be "everything," and two expressed a desire for a world where race does not matter. In that vein, we found that one way

---

25 Renn, 2008.

this is manifested is by multiracial individuals mentioning racial identities tied to a global context. Almost all younger participants (younger than 25 years old) took this position before and after DNA testing, such as a teenager who looked at her profile and said, "I love having so many races on my profile." People who expressed this global view tended to be middle- to upper-middle-class children of professionals. Many had traveled or lived abroad. They had studied other cultures in school. One Black-White biracial young woman discussed the history of Latin America and the differences in how ethnicities integrated when Europeans came to Central and South America versus the United States. In particular, this pattern seems to apply more to middle- to upper-middle-class respondents who are able to have these experiences, perhaps because they have more life options and a wider perspective.

These participants articulated clear understanding of styles, behaviors, and histories of other parts of the world that shaped their expression of self. For some respondents, the process of **deconstructing race** from its common social construction of being heavily based on phenotype involved expressing an appreciation of having unexpected results in their DNA. This seemed to free them from the constraints of being associated only with specific races. After receiving her DNA results, one respondent in her early 20s who initially identified as Black and White said, "If I was in an in-depth conversation with someone, I will now elaborate and explain that I am mixed with a number of ethnicities. I would explain that though my parents appear to look Caucasian and African American that it has been proven that I also have many other ethnicities, and I would focus on that." These individuals seemed interested in being part of and representing a diverse world. In addition to being interested in and seeking knowledge about global diversity, other multiracial participants had either immigrant parents or grandparents and felt personal links to cultures beyond the United States. A White/Latino 9-year-old respondent whose father is Latin American talked about attitudes about soccer in Latin America, where he has visited several times. Unlike generations past, these individuals had roots in other countries, freely traveled back and forth, spoke to relatives on the phone, and did not hesitate to talk openly about where they were from. One person expressed, "I think my results are perfect because it represents so many societies and the joining and merging of so many ethnicities." Several comments were similar, such as, "My perfect background would be all races because I would have all those cultures to pull from." These people were probably the most racially flexible, often choosing not to be tied to any particular race or ethnic origin.

Not relating to a particular race in a racialized society may be problematic. A Brazilian–African American–German woman said, "When we're watching videos in school about slavery, it makes me uncomfortable. It's as if they're putting it on me because they're my ancestors. I feel sorry for what happened, but I don't relate to slaves." She resented people pegging her simply because of her skin color. Adding to her complexity, this young woman had a mother who identifies as German and Latina and a father who is African American. She mentioned that her father's mother has often said, strangely, "My son is married to some Korean woman." When the mother (who was also tested and interviewed) had a DNA profile that came back with a high percentage of Asian descent, everyone (except, perhaps, the mother-in-law) was baffled. All wondered what the mother-in-law was seeing in her daughter-in-law all these years. The revelation expanded an already demanding racial narrative for the daughter, but she readily embraced it as another element of complexity in her multiracial reality.

Distinguishing Between Race and Culture

This perspective gives the individual authority to claim a culture and identification even if a DNA link is not expected or found. For instance, a Chinese child adopted into a White American family may identify as White because of lived experience, but is often given authority by non-Chinese to speak about the Chinese culture and may feel pressure from culturally Chinese to behave or feel in certain ways reflective of Chinese norms. About half of respondents used this pattern of articulation, concurrently mixing and matching their racial and cultural identities. This happened quite a bit when DNA results did not have a racial profile that they expected but they felt they owned because they had lived experience in that culture. Participants who articulated identification that fell into the second or third patterns discussed previously often also brought this pattern into their identity narrative. Often, their identification not only shifted among their racial DNA categories but also included their culture and lived experiences.

One person explained that she loved Latinx culture but pulled from her majority White lived experience a certain feeling of entitlement that she did not see in her Latinx peers. Still, she retained what she valued from the Latinx culture, such as the warmth of people, the language, family orientation, and food:

> "I look very White and my dad (from Ecuador) traveled a lot so I spent more time with my mom (who is White). I would say I'm culturally White. ... I'm not sure if it's so much race as culture. You could say, I mean it could be, culture is probably almost synonymous. My dad (from Ecuador) has a much more group-oriented culture. So first is family, as I'm not sure if my mom has told you any of this story but the dynamic of the mother-in-law, the parent, the in-law dynamic, it's a cultural difference in Ecuador and South America. It's customary for, I know especially, well I mean I can't speak for other South American cultures, but in Ecuador it's customary for the ... parents of the newlyweds to be present for the honeymoon. And the newlywed couple goes to visit family on their honeymoon. It's what my parents had to do when they got stuck with my grandma and grandpa from Ecuador, and my parents had to chaperone them and take them around New York for 2 weeks instead of going on their honeymoon. And my *abuelo*, my dad's father, suggested that they all share a hotel room on the very first night when they got to New York because they wanted to save on costs. My mom was like 'What?'"

A multi-ancestry DNA profile confirmed her distinction between a rich culture and a racial background that was not tied to a single group. Especially when an already multiracially identified person finds that their ancestry profile is not the neat breakdown predicted (half Chinese and half African, for example), they feel most compelled to articulate the race–culture distinction.

Some respondents wanted to claim a cultural identity more fully because it showed up as part of their genetic background. One woman talked about interest in joining the club for students of color in college because she was invited, being "half Black." She said that she felt welcome, but that never fully happened because she did not relate emotionally. Her DNA profile just further complicated her sense of race because it had more Middle Eastern than African results, but she (a biology major) said this was likely her more distant ancestry, and she did not relate to that at all culturally and could not identify as such because it was not part of her lived experience.

The DNA results of another respondent who initially identified as African American and Native American showed 98% African and no Native American. However, because of her family experience in Native American culture, she continued to identify as both, even if not everyone in her family did.

> "I think that was just a cultural thing. In fact, my dad is the chief of the Nanticoke tribe. My oldest sister feels very much that because a lot of the Native Americans back then didn't want any of the darker skin Indians in the Nanticoke tribe, that we shouldn't identify with them at all because [of] that rift … whatever happened in the tribe. My mother passed in July, but she was the same way. She would help with the powwows, and cook and stuff, but she would never officially join the counsel because she always felt like they had alienated and segregated themselves and she just couldn't quite get past that."

This perspective can give insight regarding a person like Rachel Dolezal, who we discuss in Chapter 6, the sensationalized case of an American woman born into a White family, who became ensconced in African American culture and community. She ultimately changed her looks and began to call herself biracial and African American. When confronted, she described herself as genetically White and culturally Black, clearly implying that her lived experience, or culture, was equally if not more salient than her biological ancestry. Many in the African American community found her story offensive, but this study suggests that this might happen more often than one might suspect. The fact that she felt that she had to "perform" a Black identity by changing her physical appearance and creating a personal narrative is intriguing. There is a perceived price to pay when one does not have genetic authority, which is why finding no ancestry in the area with which one has always identified is also anxiety provoking.

Multiracial people do seem to offer some insight into a world where racial lines are accepted as fuzzy and where racial profiles and stigma are challenged even within oneself.

Changes in world communication, travel, migration, and social, political, and economic dynamics, as well as changes in racial categorizations per se and direct-to-consumer DNA testing, which continues to advance,[26] are leading to more complex ways mixed-race individuals choose to identify and how they articulate this. Direct-to-consumer DNA has pushed people to the edge of their racial classifications. It provides an additional layer of information to consider in how they choose to identify themselves, a process that involves a myriad of factors such as phenotype, social class, language spoken, family narratives, and peer relations.

This work leads to three conclusions regarding the link between direct-to-consumer DNA and the racial identity of multiracial people. First, adding new DNA information further muddles the neat categories of race, consistent with new articulation of race based on genetic data[27] and the view of race as socially construct-ed.[28] Second, for multiracial individuals, it emphasizes fluidity of identification theorized by researchers such as Renn.[29] Third, and relatedly, even for people who identify as multiracial, it challenges the neat percentages they tend to associate with their backgrounds. Particularly for younger multiracial individuals who were pre-sented with this more fluid image, it gave them less of a sense that race was a real thing and more of a sense that culture played a big part in how they saw themselves.

It is interesting that many multiracial people seem to have developed a comfort with a narrative that functions in the con-text not only of their DNA but also of culture and experience. Yet, since many of them already challenge society's conception of race, they will probably continue to expand their articulation of self, leading the way to new views of race and perhaps comfort with the idea of racial ambiguity. The potential clearly exists and has been noted by others who are exploring ancestry DNA data

---

26 Sudmant et al., 2015.
27 Hirschman & Panther-Yates, 2008; Hochschild et al., 2012.
28 Richeson & Sommers, 2016.
29 Renn, 2008.

and race.[30] Our exploration of how genotype information affects identification narratives of multiracial individuals concludes with a finding that multiracial individuals, especially younger ones, use new DNA information to add texture and depth in talking about their identities. Their increased flexibility may push society as a whole toward more complicated views of race, although the process is slow and certainly not straight or unidirectional.

All of this brings up the point that narratives of race are in transition and that this is only highlighted among people who have already pushed the boundaries of race. Narratives are important—and not just narratives of family and culture but also genetic narratives. Multiracial individuals view all of these narratives to be valid in how they see themselves, and they are at the forefront of questioning societal limitations and impositions on how they claim and articulate their race. One could make a case that the world is surely in need of expanded narratives regarding race.

DISCUSSION QUESTIONS

1. In your experience, do older and younger people have different attitudes toward race in the United States?

2. Do you think it is okay for someone to claim a race or ethnicity even if it is not on their profile, as long as they have grown up in that culture?

3. Has your race ever been misidentified? How did it feel?

4. Explain a way that you do not fit in neatly to your culture.

ACTIVITIES

1. Write a summary of your day and explain what might be different if you were identified as a different race, sex, ability,

---

30 Hirschman & Panther-Yates, 2008; Hochschild et al., 2012.

gender, and so on. What category did you select and why? Were you fearful at any point in the scenario?

2. What, if anything, would be surprising to find in your background? In groups, see if you have a person who does have that background and compare your perceptions of what aspects of that culture are central.

LEARN MORE

What Does Our DNA Tell Us?

Web Link: https://tinyurl.com/y2axhzyw

5

SECRETS, SURPRISES, AND GENES

Where Did *That* Come From?

"A lie becomes the truth"

—Michael Jackson, "Billie Jean"

"Who are you going to believe, me or your lyin' eyes?"

Attributed to many, including Groucho Marx

I've got a secret. And, I'll bet you do too. And some people take their secrets to the grave. Some secrets stay buried there, but others are unearthed and can cause great upheaval when revealed. This chapter is about secrets, gaps, and downright lies that bear on identity in the age of direct-to-consumer DNA testing.

The next two chapters work in tandem. They include six case examples of **contested identity**. Chapter 5 looks at three instances in which people are primarily discovering unknown information based on direct-to-consumer DNA testing. Chapter 6 focuses more on people who feel an affinity for a group that others question their claim to. We unpack each case using theory and perspective presented earlier in the book to help you think about how to apply these theories in real life for insight. These cases are inspired by participants in the DNA project, but they are not their word-for-word stories. We include photographs of the inspirational person when we were given permission.

We will leave it to you to decide if people have good reasons for their decisions and in each case what would be the right thing to do. We present these cases for your consideration.

Kara's Narrative Proof

All her life people have told Kara that she looks Asian. Kara has straight dark hair, dark bright eyes, and rich clear skin. She always said that it was because of her Italian heritage. Still, often people assumed she had Asian background; some asked her outright. Her response was always, "No, no, no, I'm just a plain old White person." When she asked her parents on several occasions if they had any Asian in their families, they too said no, just southern European. Since Kara had no reason to disbelieve her parents, she accepted their explanations. Kara, by nature, was a rather happy-go-lucky, make no waves kind of person and not one to obsess, so when this issue came up time and time again, she repeatedly let it go.

Then, Kara took a direct-to-consumer DNA test, "just out of curiosity." Her profile came back as 50% East Asian. Korean. *What?!* Kara immediately confronted her father. His response was matter of fact. "Well if you are half Asian, then Jim Kane is your biological father." *What?!* Who the hell was Jim Kane? And what kind of name was that for someone Korean?

Turns out that Jim Kane was a Korean man. He had been adopted as a child by a White family who was unable to have biological children. He had known Kara's mother when he lived in the neighborhood for a brief period of time. Obviously Kara's mother had had sex with him. To this date, the circumstances are unclear, but both Kara's mother and father swear that it never occurred to them he might be Kara's biological dad.

As unbelievable as Kara's story may seem, the key elements presented here are true. Using Fisher's narrative paradigm, we can analyze Kara's story to see how narrative functions and traditional narratives can unravel in the face of new convincing ancestry information.

You will recall from Chapter 2, theorist Walter Fisher builds his narrative theory on the belief that humans are "storytelling animals."[1] These stories carry not only our facts but our hopes and values. They give our lives stability and meaning. In a 2009 publication *Science and Magic*, I make the point that

---

1   Fisher, 1985, 1989.

human beings and DNA often have incompatible, even competing goals. DNA has only the agenda of taking itself forward. It is neutral on issues of race, rape, subterfuge or social convention. People, on the other hand, have a desire for a unified, utilitarian, and identity supporting narrative. Two people's lives can touch briefly for the most random, unacceptable, or dire of reasons and the DNA imprint defines all subsequent generations and is part of their very essence ... forever.[2]

This being the case, a narrative can be in competition with DNA science. Two truths come into conflict. According to Fisher, for a story to be successful, it must meet two standards of narrative proof: narrative coherence, that the story holds together, and narrative fidelity, that it rings true. This is not the same as the scientific logic of **objectivity** and the **systematic scrutiny**. In narrative, a story does not have to be objectively true to be believed and what is objectively true is not always believed.

For Kara, the established story of her family was (almost!) completely coherent and one that fit the American narrative. Her family was nuclear; her parents were both White, married, and the children were born in the context of that wedlock. Such a story is so woven into the American ideal that there would be little reason to ever question it and every reason to reinforce it.

The fidelity of the story is slightly more tenuous. Kara reports that even as a small child people asked if she was adopted. People look at her baby pictures and say that she looks like a "little buddha." But with no motivation to question, an acceptable scientific explanation is to insist that her background (southern European) is consistent with her phenotype (how she looks). Long before direct-to-consumer DNA testing was available, people have known about the mix of genetic matter from two parents and the diversity that mix can create in offspring. Siblings can look quite different from one another and from either parent. In one of our DNA Discussion Project sessions, a set of fraternal twins attended (whom we have yet to test). The sister is tall and blonde, and the brother is short and dark. Not only do the two have to convince

---

2   Foeman, 2009.

people they are twins but that they are siblings at all! Fortunately, the twins have all kinds of photos (including an ultrasound) and family lore to support their story.

Given a powerful narrative, scientific data has to be very authoritative to break through. The key to the maintenance of some weak or weakening narratives may be strategic ignorance. In Kara's case, until presented with DNA data, there was no true evidence but her phenotype, which was ambiguous, and Kara's parents gave her no additional facts. One has to wonder how it is at all possible that Kara's mother would not suspect that Jim Kane was Kara's biological parent. Kara's mother has to have known that she had sex with Jim. And how much denial had to be involved for Kara's father to accept it, especially since he knew the name Jim Kane immediately when confronted.

In any narrative, certain elements are sharpened, some elements are softened or altered (if the alteration passes narrative muster), and other elements seem to fade into our backgrounds, are deemed not necessary or otherwise disposable. Had Kara's mother and father discussed the situation privately and decided consciously to keep the nature of the pregnancy a secret? Did they collude unconsciously? What was the nature of the sexual encounter between Kara's mother and Jim? Had there been other infidelities? Might there be questions about other siblings' paternity? Even though people outside of the family questioned, they were probably not invested in unearthing "the truth." There was more pressure within the family to maintain the narrative than from outside to change it—until Kara busted the system open.

There are many stories that have been in the popular media (and in our project) where through direct-to-consumer DNA testing individuals have discovered that one (generally the father) or both parents were not related to them. The most comprehensive study of false paternal identification is a 2006 study published in *Current Anthropology* that estimates that people who have high paternity confidence are wrong about 2% of the time.[3] In 2020 Bryan Sykes (one of the originators of ancestry genetics) and Catherine Irven, both of the Institute of Molecular Medicine at the University of Oxford, conservatively estimate nonpaternity rate at 1.3%. Some

---

3   Anderson, 2006.

estimates are much higher.[4] While 1–2% percent seems meager, that is a lot for people who are incorrectly identified as the father. Of course, a much smaller percentage of this group are of a different racial background than the biological father. And it would seem that this situation would be much more difficult to explain away. Clearly, it does happen in some instances. It is likely even more difficult to absorb.

As we have mentioned earlier in the text, researchers have found that it is uniquely difficult to discover personal ancestry that is of a different racial group.[5] And in Kara's case both the paternity and the race are changed. Is finding that one is Asian rather than White especially jarring? Our participants found Asian ancestry most surprising of all. Would Kara have felt differently had the race been African or Middle Eastern instead of Asian?

Without a doubt, this information has rocked Kara and her family's world. Kara has connected with her biological father. The two related immediately. Kara discovered that while her biological father's name is Jim Kane, he did not grow up with his White family. When his adopted mother became pregnant when he was about 4 they returned him to the orphanage. This was only one of a series of horrors in Jim Kane's life. Yet, he is a can-do, buoyant person, much like Kara. They are now in regular contact, and they even vacation together. Kara's adopted dad is not happy.

Kara is a media professional who reached out to the DNA Discussion Project as she was developing a project around finding relatives of a different race. She is in a great position to tell her own story and the complex stories of other DNA participants she has come across in her work.

Olive's Multiracial Stages

Olive Persad grew up during a time and place in the United States where people were either Black or White. Olive was Black. She grew up in a middle-class, integrated neighborhood at a time when many of the first African Americans to integrate were of the lightest complexion. Olive, with her light brown skin and big curly hair,

---

4   Sykes & Irven, 2000.
5   Roth & Ivemark, 2018.

looked like her African American peers. Olive's house was one of the hubs of activity. All kinds of kids from the neighborhood passed through her house and felt welcomed. While some parents openly and negatively commented on the skin color, hair texture, or occupation of other kids and their parents, and actively fed into the race hierarchy (light skin and straight hair were at the pinnacle), Olive's parents did not.

Olive's dad was a minister of a small African American church when the civil rights movement was strong. He hosted several civil rights speakers at his church. Olive's mom was always around and about. Few kids would have known if she worked or at what. This was a time when families were defined by the father's job. In fact, one of their friends had two parents who were both physicians. People always referred to the dad as Dr. and the mom as Mrs., and, honestly, most people assumed she was a nurse. She never once corrected that assumption.

Although Olive identified as Black, the fact is her father was of Indian (India) descent. He was born in the Caribbean and was likely a descendant of the India diaspora that wound up in the Caribbean as servants to the British colonizers. Olive's mom identified as Black. This was the time of "one drop." She was a very light-skinned woman who was adopted and raised by a very dark-skinned, loving, African American mother. In her later years, Olive says that her mom retired to an assisted care community and, as Olive describes it, "Everyone just assumes that she is one of the many little Jewish ladies there."

Olive's story can be unpacked exploring the categories of racial identification presented in original research by the authors and reviewed in Chapter 4 of this text. In this work, we interviewed people who identify as multiracial. This means that their parents or grandparents were of different racial backgrounds. We also noted in this research that the racial language used by interviewees such as, "I am half Black and half White," was often misleading because many people over many generations have mixed for a variety of reasons, but have never identified as multiracial, so most people do not really know their full ancestry, and certainly not past one or two generations back. We further predicted in this research that the attitudes of these self-identified multiracial people likely represented the vanguard in terms of the direction in which racial attitudes are moving in the United States, especially given new data coming from direct-to-consumer DNA tests.

In our research, we identified four patterns in how these people articulated identity. First, some identified as a single race, despite knowing that their parents were of different races. Second, some articulate one identity, but this can shift in response to various conditions, like an attack on the secondary identity. Third, some people opt out of any traditional categories applied to race. Finally, some people distinguish between traditional categories of race and culture and own the two identities in different ways. We found that adding new direct-to-consumer DNA information to the mix further muddles the neat categories of race, consistent with the view of race as socially constructed. Our results emphasize the fluidity of identification for multiracial individuals, and we predict that direct-to-consumer tests will highlight the multiracial nature of many more people and challenge how we all see race, over time, moving us in the direction of self-identified multiracial people we interviewed. This will be particularly true for younger individuals, for whom there was less of a sense that race was a valid marker.

Olive is now in her 60s and has children in their 20s and 30s. Consistent with our findings, Olive fits squarely in the first category of our research. She identifies as one race, Black and only Black. When asked if she felt misrepresented because people did not acknowledge that she had several cultures in her background (Caribbean, Indian, European, as well as African) that were not acknowledged, her response was, "Not at all. I wanted to be treated like I was Black. And I was." Asked if she questioned her dad about his background, she said, "No, not really," despite the fact that Olive was very close to her father. Olive did say that she has Indian relatives who are not very supportive and often behaved distant toward them growing up. So, to some extent, it was the African American community who owned Olive and she owned them. In a racial hierarchy that placed Whites at the top and Blacks at the bottom, this identification is consistent with the theory of hypo-descence, which predicts that a mixed-race person will generally be identified with the race of lower status.[6] Likely, Olive's Indian relations were trying to improve their own tenuous place in the

---

6   Ho et al., 2017.

racial hierarchy and feared their association with Black relations would bring them down.

Today, more young people (though not all) have more interest in diversity among their friends and relations and within themselves. New interest in multiracial identification, as well as movements against colorism, can hopefully move society forward.

The second category on multiracial identification that our research suggested involved individuals who might identify as one category but could shift in different situations. They might either toggle back and forth in different circumstances (like with family members of different races) or find that an identity was invoked under particular conditions (like a biracial person who mostly passes as White but gets angered when a White peer makes a racist comment). Despite Olive's identification as Black and the early attitudes of her Indian relatives toward her, Olive confirms that she would speak out if someone made negative comments about Indians and would feel that it was a direct slight to her family. Notably, the younger generation does not carry the same standoffish manner, which may again reflect a generational divide.

We met very few people in our research or in Olive's story who would identify with the third category of being simply multiracial or extraracial. Olive's profile across three continents could certainly qualify her for such an identification. When Olive looked at her DNA profile she was shocked: 45% Southern Asia and an additional 6% from Western or Central India, 24% Jewish, 22% African ancestry from diverse areas of the continent (see Figure 5.1). Her mother says that the Jewish ancestry is likely from her father, Olive's grandfather. It may have something to do with why she was put up for adoption. Thus, on both sides, Olive's family is defaulted to the lower social status, which on both sides is Black. Olive, and many other people who identify as Black, are left with a rainbow of ancestries and a singular identification, African American.

It is hard to imagine many of Olive's generation in the United States conceptualizing their own race in an uncategorized or non-racial way. The closest we have come would be Latinx individuals who have acknowledged family members of every complexion and multiple backgrounds. They even accept people as "honorary Latinx." Perhaps this identification will be more common among generations yet to be born.

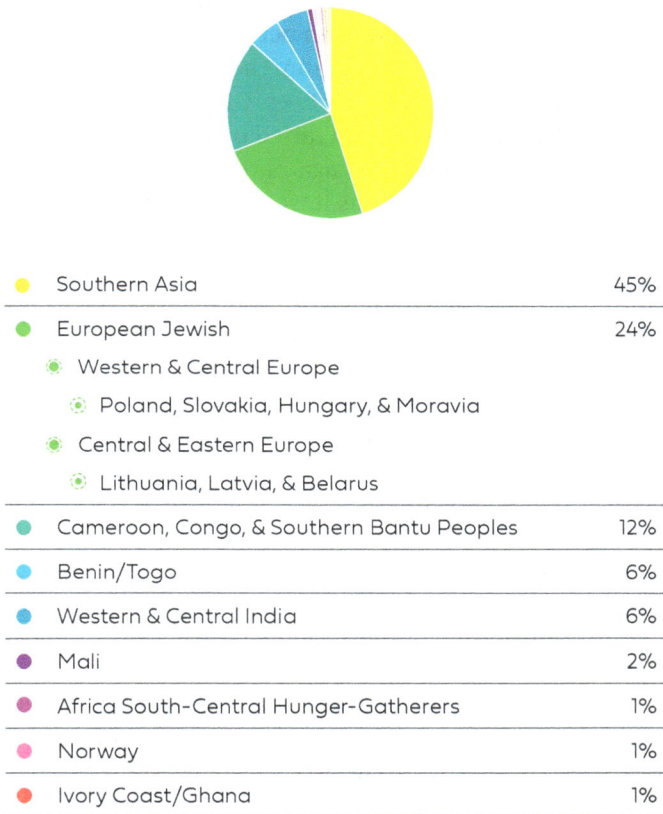

● Southern Asia	45%
● European Jewish	24%
☀ Western & Central Europe	
☀ Poland, Slovakia, Hungary, & Moravia	
☀ Central & Eastern Europe	
☀ Lithuania, Latvia, & Belarus	
● Cameroon, Congo, & Southern Bantu Peoples	12%
● Benin/Togo	6%
● Western & Central India	6%
● Mali	2%
● Africa South-Central Hunger-Gatherers	1%
● Norway	1%
● Ivory Coast/Ghana	1%

Figure 5.1 Ethnicity Estimate and DNA Story for Olive

Our last category explains that some people distinguish race from culture and hope to access their range of ancestries despite a racial identification. It is not the same as the distinction between race and ethnicity. These people may or may not see an ancestry as their established ethnic background, but they access and own elements as their culture as it resonates with them (food, or humor, or interests, etc.). Olive's children are interested in the background and culture of their grandfather, and they question Olive about it often. And people in our research of all races had more interest in finding diversity in their backgrounds and determining how it came into their families and what traces were left. Identifying as Black themselves, Olive's children actually relate to the fourth category, in which they distinguish between race and culture and feel an authenticity in borrowing from their Indian/Caribbean culture and making that part of their lives. Olive's mother, perhaps of Jewish and African ancestry, and raised by a Black woman, might have made that distinction, but, again, there would not have been a context for this view in her life. It would be interesting to explore how many older people would like to go back and unearth lost paths. We commonly come across older people who are sad that they never learned the language of their parents and grandparents, having grown up in a time when speaking English and only English was one of the costs of being an American.

We have referenced several times in this book the factors that have worked to soften attitudes about race. These include movements to alleviate colorism, increasing immigration, multicultural studies and genetic testing. In our research, we did find that the younger generation was more open to a more flexible attitude toward race. Legal change like *Loving v. Commonwealth of Virginia*,[7] multiracial people like Latinxs, global mobility, and other factors will continue to change racial makeup of the United States faster than ever before in human history. It is a trend that some have resisted but is impossible to stop. As we uncover the stories of people like Olive, we can open ourselves to understand and acknowledge the diversity in us all.

Derick's Stigma

Derick took the direct-to-consumer DNA test one January because he wanted to find his biological father. He is also interested in his specific ancestral lines. Derick is 40 years old and was helping organize a test cohort for DNA Discussion project research. Derick holds an administrative position at a historically Black university partnering with West Chester University in a project. Derick has felt somewhat untethered his entire life. He grew up in the foster care system where he was beaten and molested. His mother abused drugs and died young. As if this were not enough to manage, Derick

---

7 *Loving v. State of Virginia*, 1967.

is a gay Black man who is also deeply religious. Derick's life can be viewed through many lenses of identity. Applying Goffman's theory of stigma and Hecht's communication theory of identity (CTI), both cited in Chapter 1 of this text, we can gain insight into Derick's experience and how he hopes that a DNA test can help him find answers to questions to satisfy his need to define himself. At present, some of Derick's identities are in conflict with one another, some of his identities intersect in a synergistic way, and some of his identities carry stigma in society. All are tied to his sense of manhood.

It is important to know at the outset that Derick is one of the kindest, most sincere and open individuals you will ever meet. No one would fault him for being an angry, maladjusted mess, but he is the opposite. One of the questions, especially given his mother's emotional state, is if there is something about his father that is genetically predisposed toward resilience—that and the obvious question as to why he was never part of Derick's life.

In American society, there are few more stigmatized people than a fatherless Black boy with a drug-addicted mother. And although it is a virtual trope in song and film, it is Derick's life. Erving Goffman introduces his discussion of stigma stating that "society established the means of categorizing persons and the complement of attributes felt to be ordinary and natural for members of each of these categories."[8] In Derick's case, almost all of the defining attributes are negative: anger, criminality, ignorance. Goffman defines stigma as "deeply discrediting."[9] For sure, it is almost impossible to overestimate how deeply negative and ingrained the social stigma is for a boy like Derick. This is what Goffman calls Derick's "social identity,"[10] and what Hecht would describe in CTI as Derick's "communal" identity."[11] You may recall that Hecht views identity as operating on four levels, personal (individual), enacted (performed), relational (between people), and communal (societal). Hecht predicts that gaps in identity within or across levels can have negative outcomes for an individual. As Hecht

---

8 Goffman, 1964, p. 11.
9 Ibid., p. 13.
10 Ibid., p. 11.
11 Hecht, 1993, p. 80.

would predict, at times these identities and gaps have been a great source of distress for Derick.

For a period, Derick as an individual did embody much of what society expects of a child in his circumstance. He was angry and overwhelmed, and his performance reflected this. Derick says that his saving grace was meeting his foster (later adoptive) parents. He adopted their religion as well and, in that loving care, found support and a new possibility for how to define himself relationally, as part of a family, albeit, not a biological one.

But even in that setting Derick was sexually abused by his adoptive brother, 20 years his senior. This brought Derick a great deal of shame. It also forced him to confront feelings about the possibility that he was gay, long before he was able to understand or assert his own independent sexual identity. Derick wonders if his attraction to men is because of this early sexual contact or if perhaps his foster brother saw something in him that attracted him to Derick—nature or "nurture," who knows. When Derick confronted his abuser as an adult himself, the older brother talked about his own sexual shame and how he saw their "relationship" as loving. Confusingly, Dereck sees that aspect as well.

At some point, Derick says, in the midst of all his many challenges, he made the conscious decision that he would refuse to continue to identify himself as a victim, and instead see himself as a survivor. This change in personal identity was like a light switch for him, and it is unclear exactly what precipitated it.

To a large extent, Derick does see his adoption of religion as his literal salvation. His feeling that he was precious to a loving God was transformative. But with this salvation also came very strong sanctions against his attraction to men. He considered if his feelings were a choice that he can change, ignore, or reject, or if it is a part of him that springs directly from his biological make-up. In any case, Derick struggles to reconcile these two parts of his "self."

Unpacking many of his complicated personal identities is difficult: victim, survivor, Black, gay, foster child, adopted child, child of God. How many of these aspects could be understood by finding his biological father?

Derick's stigmas fall into two of Goffman's categories, alignment (what group he is part of), and moral character (his actions). Derick was born Black and poor, and that intersection has made his life especially hard. He is also gay, which is often identified by people who disapprove of "the gay lifestyle" as a choice of how to act or perform. It is seen as stigma associated with his moral character. Derick's gay and Black identities also intersect in unique ways.

The idea of nature or nurture is important because, on some level, most of society seems to understand that it is unfair to stigmatize a person for something over which they have no control. Being gay in the Black community, in Derick's experience, is still often seen as a sin, and an intolerable failing, although there have always been whispers of the beloved "gay choir director" and the like. And some people have suggested that Derick might perform one identity in public and another in his private life on the "down low" (specifically, getting married or being in traditional relationships while having gay relationships covertly).

For now, Derick feels that his best choice is to be celibate. He feels that this is a preferable option partly because of how sex was used in a manipulative way in his own life. While he won't lie about himself, he is "discreet." He does support gay friends and hopes that in his role as one of the religious leaders in his church he can help change attitudes about being gay and Christian. He is not totally comfortable with the compromise he has chosen, and his bargain has placed a strain on some of his relationships.

To many today, it may seem strange to debate if a person can choose to be gay or if we should discriminate against someone for something that may be a state of birth. But, consider past religious speculation by some White Christians that Blackness was a curse posed on the African race as descendants of a biblical figure in the Book of Genesis, Ham, whose genetic line was cursed because he looked on his father's nakedness.[12] The idea of carrying a genetic mark for moral failings is not new.

While Derick has mixed feelings about his sexuality, he is unequivocally a proud Black man. In addition to looking to the DNA test to locate his father, Derick was excited about seeing his ancestry profile and to learn what parts of Africa are in his background.

On a final note, among all of Derick's complex identities is his education. Occasionally, Derick's academic achievements have

---

12 Goldenberg, 2016.

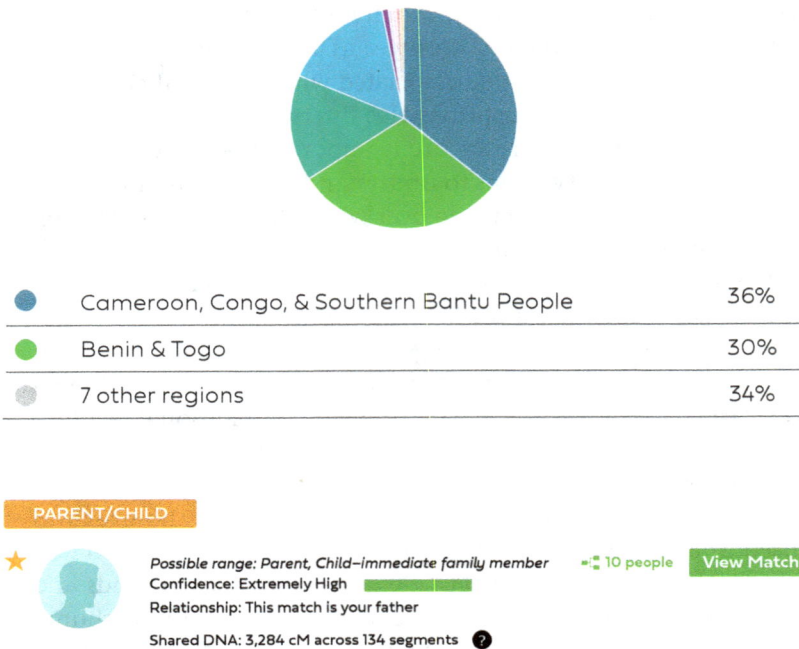

●	Cameroon, Congo, & Southern Bantu People	36%
●	Benin & Togo	30%
●	7 other regions	34%

PARENT/CHILD

Possible range: Parent, Child–immediate family member   ⬩⁝ 10 people   **View Match**
Confidence: Extremely High
Relationship: This match is your father

Shared DNA: 3,284 cM across 134 segments ❔

Figure 5.2 Derick's DNA Story and Possible Parent/Child Relationship.

separated him from some of the people in his past when he chose to pursue education and those around him ridiculed his hard work. These complex intersections of sexual identity, race, religion, and class are powerful and have been explored in scholarly literature.

Communication and performance scholar Bryant Alexander talks about the conflicts that press on the personal, enacted (performed), relational, and communal identities of a person like Derick, threatening his very manhood on multiple levels.[13] Alexander deconstructs that as a gay man in the Black community Derick is seen as weak and thus not a *real* man. As a proud, educated Black man Derick is seen as a *threat* in the White community. He was also a threat as a violent Black boy. Indeed, Goffman identifies the only acceptable option for a Black man in White society is that of loveable clown. This is a nonthreatening performance for a gay

---

13 Alexander, 2004.

man as well, but not for Derick. Also, as an academic, Derick is sometimes seen as wanting to be White, thus an *inauthentic* Black man. Add to that, that Derick is not even a real gay man or a real Christian man. The gaps of identity could be overwhelming. Alexander describes it as a constant "state of being between … performance communities":[14] always trying to pass, never being just right, always living with the risk of being outed. And yet, Derick's overarching identity is that of a survivor and a role model to most people who know him. Is this despite his challenges? Because of them, irrelevant to them? Where do the answers lie?

In early March, Derick received notice that his ancestry results had come in. Derick immediately went online to see his ancestry profile and his links. The pie chart that popped up first showed 97% African ancestry from all along the west coast of Africa. His ancestors came from Cameroon, Congo, and Southern Bantu peoples, plus Benin and Togo and seven other regions. Wow. Derick also saw that he had quite a number of fairly close relative matches. Clicking on this link he immediately saw a first and last name of a person and next to it:

> Possible range: Parent, Child–immediate family member
> Confidence: Extremely High
> Relationship: This match is your father

It was a name that Derick had never seen before. Derick was stunned. After he caught his breath, he logged in and looked at this link on the site. The person had not logged in for over a year. He looked on Facebook and found a person with this name. The man appeared to be a leader in his religious community. But that Facebook site was dormant too. After a lot of sleuthing, Derick was able to identify and e-mail a cousin of this man to ask if she would reach out to him. In response, the cousin sent several questions for Derick to answer about where he was from and his mother. Derick sent the answers along with his phone number. In the beginning of June, Derick's phone rang. After 40 years, the voice on the other end of the phone said, "The word on the street is that you have been trying to get in touch with me, son."

---

14 Ibid., p. 380.

This man had no prior idea that Derick existed, but he did remember a brief relationship with his mother when he was in military service. The father was completely accepting of him and overjoyed to find him. He tells Derick that his 80-year-old grandmother is excited too. He is the oldest of her grandchildren. Derick no doubt is at the beginning of a major transformation of his identity and perhaps some new insight as to some lingering questions.

DISCUSSION QUESTIONS

1. For your family, what is something that would be stigmatizing, for example being pregnant out of wedlock, having a mental illness, or being in prison?

2. If you had to guess, what do you think Kara's parents knew about the circumstances of her conception?

3. Should Kara now begin to identify herself as biracial? Would you?

4. Do you think it is as jarring to find that your race has changed as your biological parent?

5. Do you have family members who are barely acknowledged? What is this rejection based on?

6. Overall, do you think it is good or bad that people can find their biological parents by taking direct-to-consumer DNA tests? Do you think most people want to be found?

7. Are being religious and gay incompatible?

8. Do you think meeting his biological father will help Derick answer any of his questions? Which ones?

ACTIVITIES

1. Share a story that is told regularly in your family, perhaps at social gatherings. Dissect the story and explain what you think is the purpose in retelling the story.

2. Look online and find an article or a blog where a person talks about finding unexpected information from direct-to-consumer DNA tests. Identify the ways that this new information may have changed their identity.

LEARN MORE

Dealing With Unexpected Discoveries After DNA Tests

Web Link: https://tinyurl.com/y5yocroj

CREDITS

Fig. 5.1: Copyright © by Ancestry.com.

Fig. 5.2: Copyright © by Ancestry.com.

6

POSERS

Is Our Ancestry Destiny?

"Whither thou goest, I will go; and where thou lodgest, I will lodge: thy people shall be my people, and thy God my God: Where thou diest, will I die, and there will I be buried"

> —Ruth 1:15–16. Ruth swears loyalty to her mother-in-law, Naomi, whose culture she has adopted.

"Mimicry is not solidarity."

> —Tim Wise in response to Rachel Dolezal who claimed transracial identity as an African American woman.

Can we ever claim membership in a group with whom we have no genetic link? Are we bound to our genetic past? In this chapter, we will use theory presented in earlier sections to first explore two situations where people find themselves at odds with how society views them or how they have seen themselves before direct-to-consumer DNA has become part of their stories. The last case we unpack is the famous case of Rachel Dolozel who refers to herself as a "transracial person."

Aaron's Cultural Contract

Aaron Goldstein is Catholic. He attended 12 years of Catholic school. He attended CCD classes. He was confirmed. He goes to mass somewhat regularly. When Aaron took the direct-to-consumer

DNA test, the results came back as 50% European Jewish ancestry and Aaron was outraged. "I am not Jewish," he said. "I don't
understand this. What does it mean?"

The professor responded, "Well, any group that is segregated
from other populations can be identified genetically. It might be
your immediate family members, your extended relatives, your
ethnic community, and so on."

"But Jewish is a religion," Aaron, came back, "not a race, and
I'm Catholic."

Aaron has dark curly hair and dark brown eyes, and with a name
like Aaron Goldstein, someone could be forgiven for assuming that
he is Jewish, but is he?

Aaron's father was raised Jewish. Indeed, he had family members
who fled Germany to escape the Holocaust and some who perished
there. As the next generation, Aaron's dad was culturally Jewish
but never observed in any religious way. Aaron's grandparents were
religious Jews and had raised their five children in their tradition.
The community in which they lived was diverse, and some of the
siblings migrated toward Judaism and others were not observant,
like Aaron's dad. The parents did not make an issue of it.

Aaron's father met Aaron's mother in college. They hung out in
the same mixed crowd. They shared lots of interests in common
and both majored in English literature. She wanted to be a teacher
and he wanted to be a writer. She became a high school teacher
and he is an editor for business journals.

When the couple became engaged, neither family was especially
happy about it, particularly hers. Beyond their long-standing Irish
Catholic faith, the mom's family also lamented, "What about all
our traditions, Christmas Eve mass, Easter services, communion?
How could you consider giving that up?" That *was* unimaginable
for Aaron's mother, and she had never really thought it through.

Ultimately, the only reason Aaron's maternal grandparents
offered to support the marriage was that the couple agreed to raise
their children Catholic, as directed by the Church. Since Aaron's
dad was not that religious, he accepted their terms, and for 22 years
he lived by them. At that time, he could not have imagined that
22 years later his son would reject his Jewish heritage outright.
Aaron's dad kept it to himself, but the thought made him heartsick
and it created a wedge between himself and his family of origin.

Aaron's father's choices and Aaron's life experience can be explored based on the tenets of cultural contracts theory. Communication theorist Ronald Jackson uses cultural contracts to describe the negotiation of cultural identity. According to Jackson, there are three types of possible contracts, "ready-to-sign" characterized by the goal of **assimilation**, often presented by members of the **dominant culture** who expect others to accept their worldviews. The second is the "quasi-completed" contract, that requires **adaptation**, met by some consideration of both sides. The third is the fully "cocreated" contract, which comes as a result of a complete renegotiation of the existing social contracts. Jackson states that "the tragic reality is that most people neither understand all of the contracts they have signed nor all of the implications of having signed them."[1]

From this point of view, one can say that Aaron's maternal grandparents presented his dad with a ready-to-sign contract and gave him the choice to sign or they would walk away. Aaron's dad accepted their terms. As members of the majority culture, it was easy for this Christian family to be observant without seeming unreasonable or clannish and for them to assume that their traditions are "normal" in society and the best option for any potential grandchildren. Indeed, even if the couple did not raise their children as Christian, they could assume that the major traditions of Christianity would be recognized and endorsed throughout society. Their grandchildren would never be expected to go to school on Christmas day; messages of Easter fashion and festivity would surround them.

Back in class, Aaron goes on to say, "People say I am Jewish all the time. Really, it pisses me off. What is that about? Last year, a lot of the guys at my fraternity gave out cards before winter break. They gave everybody else a Christmas card and they gave me a card that said 'Season's Greetings,' like I am some kind of outsider. Now this, I'm Jewish. My father is Jewish, but I'm not. I just want to be Catholic like everybody else."

Aaron is just beginning to be confronted with the nature of the contract his father accepted on his behalf. By tradition, in the Jewish religion, since Jewish identity comes through the mother's

---

1   Jackson, 2002.

line and it was, in fact, his mother who made the determination about his upbringing, the decision may have seemed appropriate. In tradition, this is because only the mother's link to the child is unquestionable. But in the age of DNA, that thought may need to be revisited. And, of course, Aaron carries his father's last name and a total replica of his face. In addition, Aaron's paternal grandfather died long before he was born, and when Aaron's mother became pregnant, the only demand Aaron's dad made was to name his son after his own deceased father. This is the first sign that Aaron's dad wanted to press for at least a quasi-completed contract. Aaron's mother happily agreed.

Aaron's mother certainly has her own reasons for protecting her tradition. In addition to wanting Aaron to fit into her family and society at large, Catholics have experienced their own level of discrimination. Indeed, Catholics made their own negotiated contract epitomized by the speech on religion given by then presidential candidate John Fitzgerald Kennedy in 1960, the first Catholic to be the candidate for a major U.S. political party. In his speech, first, he is assuring:

> Judge me on the basis of my record of 14 years in Congress, on my declared stands against an ambassador to the Vatican, against unconstitutional aid to parochial schools, and against any boycott of the public schools (which I have attended myself). ... I do not intend to apologize ... to my critics of either Catholic or Protestant faith, nor do I intend to disavow either my views or my church in order to win this election.[2]

It is a careful negotiation that addresses both the fears of the majority and pride in his own tradition. What would such a negotiation look like for the first Jewish president? What assurances would that person have to make? How would this person cocreate a contract? How should Aaron cocreate a contract for his situation?

Aaron, unlike his father, has two backgrounds, two traditions. As with so many contracts presented fully formed, even when one is willing to sign, the contract cannot be fully implemented. Why is Aaron not fully accepted by his Catholic peers? Is it his name,

---

2   National Public Radio, 2007.

how he looks, his behavior? What does Aaron need to do to be acceptable to the majority? One might ask in a parallel manner, what does a Black person have to do to be acceptable to the White majority or a transgender person to be accepted by cisgenders? By definition, the power class maintains its power by its exclusivity.

Hecht, Jackson, and Pitts[3] state that quasi-completed contracts are *somewhat* negotiated. This may, to some extent, grow out of the impossibility of the Other to ever fully be subsumed into the majority. In any case, the process involves holding on to and letting go of parts of oneself as we accept or reject majority beliefs, norms, preferences, and judgments. Naming Aaron after a beloved family member was one place that Aaron's dad wanted to make a customized contract. He also maintained relationships with the culturally Jewish part of the family, albeit strained.

In our research, we have found quasi-completed contracts often among people who identify as biracial or multiracial. These people want to accept parts of the many aspects of their backgrounds, but they do not attempt to redefine race in culture. Aaron might well identify as multicultural. Similarly, Aaron, especially given his DNA profile, may need to reflect on his background in new ways. He can choose his religion, but his history is written in his DNA. He may need his father's help to rethink the possibilities and vice versa.

Hecht, Jackson, and Pitts[4] provide code-switching as an example of quasi-completed contracts by people who change their manner and behavior in different environments. It would be interesting for Aaron to reflect on whether he does this when he interacts with family on his mother's and father's sides. Does he bring something special to both of these environments of which he is unaware? Does he share foods or rituals across lines? Rather than submitting to one culture, might he represent a third way in which he can take pride and overcome his resentment and embarrassment? Would it be helpful for him to speak to other people like himself? There are many possibilities.

If Aaron is fully able to explore all of his options, he may be able to push for a novel, cocreated contract. In a world that has categorized people into neat and distinct groups, Aaron's dad may

---

3   Hecht et al., 2005.
4   Ibid.

have felt pressured to make choices that Aaron may not need to. Cocreated contracts represent openness and acceptance of other worldviews and assume that equal importance is given to all parties involved. It is hard to find examples of true cocreated contracts, especially on a societal scale. Existing power dynamics work against truly redefining the world. In our research, we found that infusing new voices helps us to reboot old assumptions about difference and allows societies to renegotiate old contracts. Aaron's circumstance embodies many of the rejuvenating elements like his youth and exposure to new ideas, like direct-to-consumer DNA testing.

Professors of government and political science Hochschild, Weaver, and Burch argue that immigration, the young, multiracialism, and genetic testing, all help to reshape reality.[5] In some cases, people who have been trapped in old ready-to-sign contracts can begrudge creating new contracts because it challenges their own complete surrender. However, Aaron's dad may be very happy to see his son rethink his identity. After all, both of Aaron's parents made decisions on his behalf that only he can make as a young adult. A DNA finding may be a catalyst for a new start.

We can wonder if Aaron will tell friends and family about the DNA findings. Will he post them on social media? Will Aaron find people of his generation less critical than he expects? All in all, while direct-to-consumer DNA cannot change the human heart, new information weakens unidimensional narratives of race and ethnicity and offers options for another kind of contract.

Ada's Identity Gaps

Ada was adopted from China. Today, she and her family live in the United States. Her parents are from Poland. The entire family speaks Polish, and that is what they speak most often at home. They eat Polish food; they are culturally Polish. Ada's parents migrated to the United States just before Ada was born. Ada was adopted at 2 weeks old. Her loving adoptive family is all she has ever known, and she adores them. From preschool on, she has attended the local schools in her suburban community. It is virtually all White. At

---

5   Hochschild et al., 2012.

school, Ada is social and well liked. She fits right in. As a teenager in her consolidated high school she met a fellow, David, a White guy, and they started seeing each other regularly. The first time Ada met David's parents, making small talk, they asked her, "So what are you?" She said, "I'm Polish." The young man's parents burst into laughter, assuming that she was being sarcastic. The moment was extremely awkward and, years later, Ada still has a hard time retelling the story in a college class in the DNA Discussion Project.

Ada's experience as she moved into adulthood can be explored meaningfully using the communication theory of identity (CTI),[6] specifically the concept of identity gaps. If we view identity in the four layers of CTI, we can consider the impact of each unique aspect: personal, enacted, relational, and communal.

The personal frame exists at the individual level. Ada, while she knows that she is genetically Asian, experiences herself as like those around her. Unless she is looking in the mirror, there is little to contradict this experience. Race rarely came up as a topic in her homogeneous neighborhood. She has always felt totally a part of things.

Coming of age in a racialized society, Ada might initially even think of herself as effectively White, and some Asians do,[7] and certainly culturally Polish. If questioned, Ada might acknowledge that she carries within her, another story, one that includes being given up for adoption out of a culture and reality that is far different than the life she knows now, but that story has not seemed relevant to her so far. She has really had no interest in exploring it.

Since Ada is deeply connected to her adoptive family and she shares their culture, that culture is enacted in many ways, from what she eats to how she speaks at home. Recall that identity is enacted in what we say and do, how we perform culture. The culture she performs is Polish. There is a little adjustment from home to school and the community, but not much. Other kids have Polish grandparents or other European ethnicities that make her feel similar to her peers. She is free to behave in ways that are familiar and comfortable to her. She has lots of opportunities to enact her Polish and White identities on a regular basis. Because she has been in her school district school so long, she has little

---

6   Hecht, 1993.
7   Zhou, 2007.

memory of the small confusion that occurred in kindergarten when she brought in pierogis on a school sharing day, many assuming that she would bring in something Chinese, but she was really too young to remember.

When she was younger, Ada's parents took her to Chinese classes, but when Ada joined several sports teams at school, she was over-scheduled, so they let her drop the classes. That, essentially, ended her parents' nod to her Chinese background. The classes were never mentioned again.

As Ada got older and moved into the larger community, more significant gaps within and between levels appeared, particularly between the more personal and enacted levels and the more social, relational, and communal levels. As Ada's world broadened, it was harder for her and her family to control her interactions with new people as she negotiated identity in new environments.

The relational level of communication focuses on interactions with other people. In many new situations Ada entered, people would want to know, "What are you?" They never accepted her initial answer. And, frankly, she did not know what to do to manage the gap between her personal identity and the identity that others seem dead set to force onto her. Fatigue over it led Ada to want to say something that was both true and satisfactory to people, but she has yet to figure that out. If she just says, "I'm Chinese," that feels like a lie and leads to more misunderstanding down the line. "I'm adopted," does not clarify the entire scenario either. Ada does not think she owes people the story of her life in any given situation. It is very frustrating that not only is her nascent Asian story now thrust into the limelight as part of her relational identity, it seems to have become the predominant one.

As Ada is confronted with new experiences, old ones come to mind. For example, Ada recalled a time in the urban Chinatown near their home when several people spoke to her in their Chinese dialects. She remembers feeling awkward and embarrassed. She also recalls speaking to her parents in Polish on the phone in front of a friend when they were small and the friend said in surprise, "You speak Korean?!" Thinking back, Ada has always felt somewhat exposed. She now recollects several times when servers in restaurants said to her parents out of the blue, "What good people you are for taking one of these children." Her parents always responded happily, "*We're* the lucky ones." One server even patted her on the head and said that she should be so grateful. The interaction with David's parents dredged up such memories.

Other small observances popped up in the back of her mind. Sometimes Ada felt that teachers thought she should do better in school (she did fine). Ada has also been in situations where people have given her credit for understanding Asian culture, when she has little experience of Asian culture at all. For example, she could not help college friends when they were ordering Chinese takeout.

The communal level has to do with the group or social interaction. If Ada was honest with herself, most people she knows think of "real" Asians (not "honorary" White Asians like herself), as the Other. But when people see her alone, not buffered by her White family or her gaggle of White friends, she is one of those Others to strangers on the street. Her own biological family was the Other, even to her. But, she wondered, couldn't people just look at her and know that she was not like them? Now, she wonders if she has been hesitant to explore her Asian past partly out of loyalty to her parents and partly to maintain a distance from that vague marginalization.

Ada's friends have always helped her fit in if she has ever expressed the slightest insecurity about whether she belonged in their community. Ada once said that she wished her hair was not so bone straight and dark, but she'd feel silly dying and perming it, like her friends. Her friends insisted that she was being ridiculous. They laughed that she was "just a little White girl like the rest of us." On one level, she was touched, but in another way the comment seemed like an odd and precarious agreement about what she could and could not explore in herself and her relation to others. It implied that she should continue to keep her personal Asian identity at a distance.

As gaps became larger and more numerous both within and across all levels of Ada's identity, she felt more and more uncomfortable. She needed congruence. As CTI theorists Michael Hecht and Lu found, "identity gaps contribute to low communication satisfaction and ineffectiveness, as well as leading to more pervasive negative health outcomes such as stress and depression."[8] Ada was in the midst of that psychological experience.

On a pragmatic level, she needed to determine how to respond to regular identity challenges with people. In this regard, her question became whether she would change her personal identity or change her way of interacting at the relational and communal level with those around her. How should she have responded to David's parents? Should she add to her story the story of her biological parents? Might direct-to-consumer DNA testing help her?

Direct-to-consumer DNA tests still tend to be weak for Asian ethnicities, but they are getting better, and tests can help people find biological relatives. Should she seek out these people? What should she tell her loving parents? Would they see her exploration as disloyalty?

One step that Ada did take was to visit the Asian American club on campus. To her surprise, a number of people at the meetings shared similar backgrounds to herself and related to her story. One girl had even attended her Chinese class from her elementary years. Ada is just beginning a new journey that has yet to be fully defined. In Ada's case, her identity gaps propelled her to seek new learning to fill in some information gaps and to consider skills to manage some social ones. Of course, we wish her well.

Rachel Dolezal's Essential Case

A Google search on the name *Rachel Dolezal* garners results, including "Family of race-faker Rachel Dolezal plead for reunion," "The story of Rachel Dolezal gets even more bizarre," and "Rachel Dolezal's parents tell her: We hope you'll get the help you need." The first paragraph of her Wikipedia profile ends, "Dolezal is known for claiming to be a Black woman while being of European ancestry and having no known African ancestry."[9]

Since Ms. Dolezal's biological family "outed" her for presenting herself as a Black woman during a family skirmish in 2014, Rachel Dolezal's life has been under scrutiny and is a study in the

---

8   Hecht & Lu, 2014.
9   Wikipedia, 2020.

persistence of racial essentialism.[10] The level of attention and outrage that swirled around Dolezal is noteworthy. Rachel Dolezal was not a national celebrity or a person of great wealth and influence, but her story riveted people and ricocheted around the country like a rocket. Her notoriety came about because Rachel Dolezal says that she is Black.

Rachel Dolezal's story *is* unique. Her parents are White Evangelicals. They fostered four African American children with whom Dolezal felt a strong connection. The parents' religious values apparently included negative attitudes about Black people, and Dolezal felt protective of her Black siblings.[11]

As a young adult, Dolezal took custody of one of her foster brothers and raised him. By all accounts she was a fine parental figure. She later married (and divorced) an African American man with whom she has a son.[12] Most people would identify her son as a Black person.

Rachel Dolezal grew up to be a civil rights activist. She received her MA degree from Howard University, a historically Black institution. During that time, there was some disagreement about a scholarship (among other things) she was promised that was later rescinded, and she sued the school for reverse discrimination, believing that the award was withdrawn when university officials discovered that she was White.[13] The case was ultimately dismissed.[14] At some point, later on, Ms. Dolezal began darkening her skin, changed her hair, and began to state that she is Black, which she says is more in line with how she feels internally. She changed her name to Nkechi Amare Diallo. She worked for 10 years for the NAACP as an effective advocate where she was known to be a Black woman until her biological family took her story public after she accused her biological brother of abuse. So, is Rachel Dolezal Black?

A Rassmusen poll reports that of 1,000 likely voters, most agreed that racial identity should be based on birth, not preference, but Black voters were less critical than others of Dolezal. Another

---

10 Kingstone, 2018.
11 Bey & Sakellarides, 2016.
12 Kingstone, 2018.
13 Ibid.
14 Lerner, 2015.

Rasmussen national telephone survey found that 63% of likely U.S. voters believed Dolezal was being deceitful by claiming she is Black, 13% disagreed, 23% were not sure.[15]

The Rachel Dolezal story gained attention around the time that Caitlyn Jenner (formerly Olympic athlete Bruce Jenner) presented herself as a transgender woman, so parallels between the two stories abounded.[16] Conservative media was quick to note the hypocrisy when some liberals who accepted Jenner's assertion that she is a transgender woman were dismissive when Rachel Dolezal claimed that she is transracial, White to Black.[17] More recently, she has used a different term, "trans-Black," saying, "Transracial, it almost sounds like I'm neutral, and I'm not neutral on political and social issues. ... If I was allowed a more complex term, I would say I'm pan-African, pro-Black, bisexual, mother, activist, artist, you know that's like too long. So trans-Black is quicker."[18]

Much has been made of the relationship between biological sex and biological race. While sex has traditionally been seen as a genetic binary XX or XY in the United States, today scientists acknowledge situations whereby sex conditions do not fit the strict dichotomy; instead, these **intersex** cases run along a continuum with the two biological extremes.[19] Race, on the other hand, has always been seen at the very least as having multiple points of departure, and people have always known that races do mix, even if that was socially unacceptable (hence, **anti-miscegenation laws**). Traditionally, "passing" from Black to White was seen as a strategic and pragmatic choice, rather than a cultural one, and some people assumed that Rachel Dolezal must have had ulterior motives for her choice.[20]

Resistance to Dolezal's race claim was swift and harsh.[21] Multiple talk show hosts confronted her, attempting to corner her into "admitting" that she is *really* White.[22] The discussion was eerily in line with our Chapter 1 discussion of evaluation of attitudes of

---

15 Rasmussen, 2015.
16 Brubaker, 2016.
17 Ibid.
18 Payne, 2017.
19 Ainsworth, 2018.
20 Brubaker, 2016.
21 Bey & Sakellarides, 2016.
22 Kingstone, 2018.

children and adults who perceive that racial groups have "an innate basis, stable category membership, and sharp boundaries."[23] White anti-racism activist and journalist Tim Wise argued that Blackness is "etched in their [African Americans'] DNA, in the cell memory passed to them by their ancestors." He concludes that "mimicry is not solidarity."[24]

In the eyes of many, no matter what she might say or do, Rachel Dolezal is White, not Black, and delusional to think otherwise. As Plato might have agreed in his assertion of essentialism (discussed in Chapter 1 of this text), Black and White are distinguishable, each with natural qualities that have a core essence that is constant within a category and different from one category to the next. You *are* the category and it is you. Any variation within one's essence is the result of an imperfect display of the essence. Variation is an aberration or weakness. Therefore, not only is Rachael Dolezal not a Black woman, but she is a weak example of a White woman as well.

Scholars who have unpacked such discussion acknowledge that it is problematic in nature. Race and gender theorists Bey and Sakellarides posit, "Blackness has heretofore operated—primarily as a static, fixed, rigidly 'known' thing characterized by sameness, to biological or blood quantum."[25] The conception actually slights people in all groups; people within a group are different from people outside of the group and people within the group are all the same.

From this perspective, one might ask if Rachel Dolezal actually accepts such an essentialist view herself in that she saw her attitudes and feelings as inconsistent with being White. Indeed, some people wish that she could serve as a White ally to help recast negative and oppressive ways that Whiteness has operated in society and her own family. Could similar questions be posed about gender and people who feel that they need to change their sex—especially when changing sex sometimes requires severe physical interventions? Alternately, is sex alteration perceived as more appropriate because misassigned sex is more of a "real" biological condition than race? Is it, paradoxically, the fluidity of race that makes race "flipping" so culturally threatening? Do we fear that

23 Zack, 2003.
24 Alternet, 2015.
25 Bey & Sakellarides, 2016, p. 37.

race could truly break down and challenge our very way of life? How do discussions of race and ethnicity or sex and gender help us understand how essentialism functions in society?

According to Bey and Sakellarides, "Blackness—despite its undeniable contractedness—carries a very real and lived visceral history that cannot be overlooked."[26] But, we can ask, what is this essential visceral history? Is there an essential Black experience?

Black History scholar Charles Johnson makes the case that the traditional Black narrative includes a family history of deportation from Africa, survival through the Middle Passage, slavery in the American South, and, for some, the northern migration.[27] He also says that the Black experience is not so singular today. Barack Obama, whose mother was White and father African, did not have this narrative. New immigrants, and people disconnected from their historical experience, may not relate to it, either.[28] We have had students in the DNA Discussion Project who say that they do not feel a direct connection to Africa or slavery. Do they have a Black experience? Did Rachel Dolezal have a Black experience?

Some have responded to the deception as their key objection to Dolezal, especially in changing her phenotype by changing her hair and skin. Changing skin and hair is a common behavior among many ethnic groups. If we scrutinize Rachel Dolezal, don't we have to scrutinize an industry dedicated to hair straightening and coloring, plastic surgery, and skin lightening, all dedicated to making a person look more European?

Finally, suppose Rachel Dolezal took a DNA test? Suppose she has "some" African ancestry? How much would she need to overcome objection? Would any amount "count" given that people have deemed her experience not adequately Black? Apparently, Dolezal claims she received a 10% African profile, but when she asked the company to make a certified record, they said those were not your results, and that she is 100% European.[29]

When the U.S. Census first allowed people to select more than one race, there were those who encouraged people who have taken DNA tests (or had known diverse ancestry) to select only Black for

26 Ibid., p. 34.
27 Johnson, 2008.
28 Hecht et al., 2005.
29 Payne, 2017.

political reasons related to distribution of resources.[30] Would these people encourage Rachel Dolezal to "check Black"?

In DNA Discussion Project sessions students grapple with these kinds of questions. One student asks, "Well, aren't we all Africans?" Another student retorted, "Now White people get to be everything, even Black. How far would I get if I said I am a White man?"

The furor over the Rachel Dolezal situation highlights the fact that race is not one thing; it is some contested combination of phenotype, performance, history, and other factors.

Ultimately, Bey and Sakellarides summarize, "Perhaps this is all to underscore two things: first, that Dolezal's Blackness throws into crisis fixed understandings of race and questions … what constitutes Blackness; and second, and perhaps more obliquely, that we are all 'passing.'"[31]

How does this feel for you? Are you "passing," or do you feel that you are "really" one thing or another?

DISCUSSION QUESTIONS

1. In your own mind, is Jewish a religion or a race?

2. How do you think Aaron's mother feels about his desire to be only Catholic?

3. What is Ada's best option for response when people ask about her heritage?

4. Can Ada resolve her identity gap? What is Ada's best strategy for managing the gap?

5. Is Rachel Dolezal Black?

6. Is transracial a valid term?

7. Would you be more willing to change your race or your sex?

8. Do you think there is a more biological basis for race or for sex? Either or neither? Does it matter?

---

30 Nelson, 2000
31 Bey & Saakellarides, 2016, p. 40.

9.   Will race disappear in the future?

10. How are race and gender similar? How are they different?

ACTIVITIES

1.   Find articles about other people who identify as transracial, like Rachel Dolezal. What qualities or experiences do they have in common with Rachel Dolezal?

2.   List five positive things and five challenges about transracial adoption.

3.   How many religions do you associate with racial or ethnic groups? Look online and find pictures of congregations. Do they fit that image?

LEARN MORE

Genetic ancestry testing

Web Link: https://tinyurl.com/y26agvlq

7

INTERSECTIONALITY

How Do My Different Identities Interplay?

"I liked the concept of Mitochondrial Eve and a mother to our population. We often undervalue the impor-tance that women and female characteristics play in giving legacy to our population and society. Women are a quiet, enduring and powerful force behind why we are all here and why we are who we are."

—Sam Smolko, 1st-year student, Honor's College, discussing the concept of an actual Mitochondrial Eve to whom all humans link.

D irect-to-consumer DNA helps us make connections across many fields that may not be immediately evident. In this chap-ter, we look back, around, and forward. We begin at the beginning, asking about direct-to-consumer DNA and the question "Who was Eve?" to help us expand views in critical gender and Afrocentric race studies. Second, we look at how the question "How can I help?" can link DNA to helping fields, in this case counselors using genograms to explore family dynamics. Finally, we explore how direct-to-consumer DNA can shed light on health issues.

Critical Gender and Race Studies: Who Was Eve?

Critical theorist Kimberlé Crenshaw presented the concept of intersectionality in 1989.[1] Intersectionality, also known as intersectional feminism, studies how overlapping identities combine to create

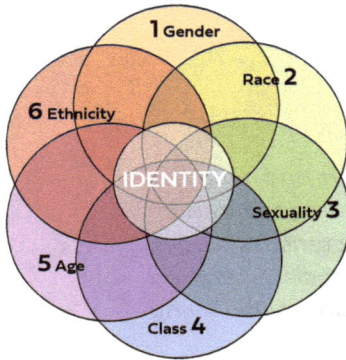

Figure 7.1 Intersectionality and assemblage: A real-life definition LGBTQ people share experiences of prejudice.

different experiences for individuals and groups (see Figure 7.1). For example, the lived experience of a White woman is often quite different from that of a Black, Latina, Indigenous, or Asian woman. Feminist scholars are constantly looking for new ways to tell diverse stories of people who do not fit the profile associated with feminism. Direct-to-consumer DNA offers such an opportunity. Finnish feminist scholar Venla Oikkonen studies cultural aspects of genetics and has specifically considered Mitochondrial Eve, sometimes called African Eve, as a figure in popular culture helping recast the intersection of race and gender in common consciousness. In her research, she examines newspaper and magazine coverage of mitochondrial DNA (mtDNA, a small part of DNA from the mother's line), tracking and examining how newly discovered ancestry connects all living people. Oikkonen explains that mitochondrial DNA is far easier to access and explore than the full human genome and the mitochondrial genome was sequenced as early as 1981, 2 decades before the completion of the Human Genome Project on which all ancestry work is based.[2] This has led to the discovery of "Eve," mother to us all. Oikkonen notes the ebb and flow of attitudes toward Mitochondrial Eve in the media that reflect conflicting attitudes about women and their changing roles in society. She explains that from the beginning, speculation about Eve brushed up against negative social attitudes about women and

---

1   Crenshaw, 1989.
2   Oikkonen, 2015.

Black women, in particular. In a 1988 *Newsweek* article entitled "The Search for Adam and Eve," journalist John Tierney writes

> Scientists are calling her Eve, but reluctantly. The name evokes too many wrong images—the weak-willed figure in Genesis, the milk-skinned beauty in Renaissance art, the voluptuary gardener in "Paradise Lost" who was all "softness" and "meek surrender" and waist-length "gold tresses." The scientists' Eve—subject of one of the most provocative anthropological theories in a decade—was more likely a dark-haired, black-skinned woman, roaming a hot savanna in search of food. She was as muscular as Martina Navratilova, maybe stronger; she might have torn animals apart with her hands, although she probably preferred to use stone tools. She was not the only woman on earth, nor necessarily the most attractive or maternal. She was simply the most fruitful, if that is measured by success in propagating a certain set of genes. Hers seem to be in all humans living today: 5 billion blood relatives. She was, by one rough estimate, your 10,000th-great-grandmother.[3]

Not attractive or maternal? What? According to what standards? Oikkonen sees this editorializing as both gendered and racialized. She further comments on the scientists' presentation of information on HeLa cells used to help track mtDNA. HeLa cells are called this because they were taken from a cancer victim, Henrietta Lacks, in the 1930s. We discuss her case in a future chapter. HeLa cells were nothing less than monumental in their positive impact on modern science. They are so important because they survive (to this day!) outside of the human body. Oikkonen reports on the scientists, saying that "the unusually aggressive growth of HeLa cells is associated with promiscuous female sexuality, which in turn is linked to women of color through the figure of Henrietta Lacks, the African American patient whose deadly cervical cancer provided—without her consent—the immortal cell line."[4]

---

3   Tierney, 1988.
4   Oikkonen, 2015, para. 33.

Figure 7.2 "I find the idea of such a founding mother endlessly mesmerizing. In human genetics, she is known by a beautiful name" —Mitochondrial Eve.[4]

The importance and exceptional nature of Lacks's cells cannot be overstated. Their exceptional distinctiveness is surely not explained by some unique promiscuity. Oikkonen sees this analysis as another expression of race and gender prejudice. So, two Black women started humanity and changed science and are cast in the most negative and disrespectful ways.

Finally, Oikkonen finds that the literature seeks to identify a parallel Adam for Mitochondrial Eve, although there is no science to warrant the same level of speculation. Adam is presented as her mate with imagined phone calls and courting, despite the fact that they did not exist at the same time.

Oikkonen summarizes that the identification of Mitochondrial Eve does offer an image "through which the underlying roles of gender, sexuality, and race in genomics may potentially be challenged."[6] In keeping with the sensibilities of critical theorists, we must constantly be vigilant in making sure that possibility is realized and that traditional stereotypes and negative images of women and people of color do not limit that possibility.

---

5   Mukherjee, 2016
6   Ibid., para. 39.

In 2016, in his book *The Gene,* oncologist, physician, and Pulitzer prize–winning author Siddhartha Mukherjee assists in moving us toward a new vision:

> If the founding population of a species is small enough, and if enough time has passed, the number of surviving maternal lineages will keep shrinking, and shrinking further, until only a few are left. ... By the end of several generations, all the descendants of the tribe, male or female, might track their mitochondrial ancestry to just a few women. For modern humans, that number has reached one: each of us can trace our mitochondrial lineage to a single human female who existed in Africa about two hundred thousand years ago. She is the common mother of our species. We do not know what she looked like, although her closest modern-day relatives are women of the San tribe from Botswana or Namibia.[7] (See Figure 7.2)

Afrocentricity: So, We Are All Africans?

The importance of race as well as gender in the Mitochondrial Eve story is obvious. That being the case, race studies, specifically **Afrocentrism**, can be supported by ancestry work. In our article "Bridging Discussions of Human History: Ancestry DNA and New Roles for Africana Studies," we state that "new genetics information places the African experience as the alpha expedience in this [the human] story. Further, the African diaspora, based on—among other things—three centuries of systematic dispersal of Black human beings that created the possibility of Western wealth, is a story reinforced by new genetics."[8] The stories of human genesis and Western wealth based on slavery and codified in the genes of those molested people place Africa at the center, which is the goal of Afrocentrism as a theoretical approach. Ancestry work can also be an important connection bringing direct-to-consumer DNA to Africana studies as a way of linking the sciences to the centrality of African people.

7   Mukherjee, 2016.
8   Lawton et al., 2018.

The fear among **Africana studies** scholars, who focus their work on African perspectives, is that new interest in Africana studies will both water down the perspective in order to make it palatable for the general population and encroach on the safe space that these programs provide for marginalized people. Another concern is that African history (much like Native American history) will be treated as part of a long-gone past. Africa is the future, and the profile of this most genetically diverse and culturally and resource-rich continent needs to be the center of conversation into the future.[9] Afrocentricity envisions this conversation as at the center rather than on the margins. Finally, the perspective that "we are all Africans" may actually undermine the Afrocentric approach. If all people can claim Africa, does the discipline get coopted by people who have little true knowledge?

The Helping Professions? Genetics and Genograms

Are there gaps in your family story? Might there be some unknown underlying dynamics in your family's past that may shape your own strengths, fears, relationships, habits? Many in the helping professions certainly think so. A genogram, also known as a McGoldrick–Gerson study, is a family tree that includes detailed information on characteristics and relationships among individuals. According to McGoldrick and her research team, "Neither people nor their problems or solutions exist in a vacuum."[10]

Male   Female   Gay   Lesbian   Transgender 1   Transgender 2   Marriage   Separation   Pet

Figure 7.3   Genogram

---

9   Ibid.
10   McGoldrick et al., 2008, p. 1.

Genograms and Direct-to-Consumer DNA

To fill in this vacuum, people and relationships are charted on the genogram using standardized notations. Developers explain that "a genogram is a modern version of a family tree that maps much more than your ancestry. It conveys who you belong to and the pattern of your family over several generations. It is by far the best way to explore and keep track of basic information about families from a systems perspective."[11]

There are **notations** for the sex and gender identity of individuals. Notations can also indicate important life events like a pregnancy or miscarriage. Notations can indicate emotional relationships, from love to hate, whether there was physical abuse, if the relationship was intense or indifferent. Health status can also be notated, and there are icons for autism, cancer, smoking, and so on. You can even indicate a pet (see Figure 7.3).

If you think about it, it makes sense that a great-grandparent born in a more conservative era and who had a pregnancy out of wedlock or as the result of an extramarital affair might spread misinformation that is carried down for generations, along with vague emotional despair to go with it. There may even be impact on the genetic level. Yet the source is unclear. Something like an interracial affair could absolutely change the trajectory of a family and create secrets that travel across time. Scholars talk about a legacy of trauma or a flow of anxiety. Yet, most people can trace back only a few generations, so lots of information have been inaccessible. In the earliest genograms, it was suggested that at least three generations be included,[12] and even that can be difficult for some people to accomplish. In the early days, the best source of information was family narrative and sometimes medical and other government records. Direct-to-consumer DNA along with the related information about family genetic relationships can extend that insight back much farther and deeper. It can reveal ancestries and heretofore unknown relationships that may have shaped family dynamics. And what better place to explore new

---

11 Ibid.
12 Ibid.

learning than with the help of a professional therapist? Even some of the testing companies are coming to this conclusion.[13]

McGoldrick and her colleagues have written extensively on ethnic culture and cultural history and their impact on our outlooks. The genogram can bring that historical awareness to the individual family system and can direct exploration. These scholars talk about "vertical" and "horizontal" dimensions.[14] The vertical axis would include a group's cultural history, for example, the **Trail of Tears**, the **Holocaust**, or the **fall of Saigon**. At the horizontal level, how prejudice presses on the individual may be an element of how personal decisions were made (like career or marriage choices). It makes sense that people in the helping professions are using direct-to-consumer DNA to fill in blanks.[15] We know from our own research in the DNA Discussion Project that people have found information that they never imagined, and for some this information provided a missing piece that gave them insight, understanding, and more emotional control.

We have noticed two things that are meaningful when people find new information. First, people are often less judgmental of relatives from generations back for their infractions. This may be because certain social attitudes have changed, but also, we find that people see the stories as more mythical. People describe their anti-social ancestors as "outlaws" or "survivors." One person was excited to find verification that she probably had pirates in her past, though it was a whispered secret for generations. One young man in the DNA Discussion Project interviewed his mother to learn about his ethnic ancestry. After some hesitation, his mother told him that his great-grandmother had been a prostitute and they had no idea who had fathered her children. He was shocked but took the story with humor—far different from the shame and scandal in her time, we are sure. When people have found unexpected relatives and behaviors it can put modern-day social complexities in a larger context. Our predecessors faced the same life trials as we do. We find that people are generally glad for the truth, and they often say that they suspected "something" and feel satisfied to know what it was. Genograms can help in this search.

---

13 Brown, 2018.
14 McGoldrick et al., 2018.
15 Family History Guide, n.d.

Genographic information informed by direct-to-consumer DNA is often uniquely helpful to adopted people in providing missing links and a health history. In DNA Discussion research we found that many respondents thought there were gaps and secrets in their backgrounds. Some individuals in our research said that the new information was life changing.

The support of a health care professional is an important element to consider with so much new genetic information now available to people. Obviously for true therapy a counseling professional may be helpful, and the genogram can be a useful tool.

One final word as we close a discussion that has focused on family dysfunction, which is often when helping professionals are called into family situations. Scholars have also found that solid genograms can be helpful across many settings, from building a strong medical history to understanding the survival strategies of our forebearers, to just learning more about who we are and expanding on one of the most popular pastimes, tracing family genealogy.[16]

Wellness: Can Direct-to-Consumer DNA Information Support My Wellness?

How would you feel about sitting in your bedroom, alone, opening your e-mail, clicking on a link, and finding out that you have a genetic predisposition for Parkinson's disease? Would you panic, call a friend, a doctor, a therapist, sink into depression, post it on social media? Would you believe it? Would that information be helpful to you? Would you want to know?

In 2013, the Food and Drug Administration (FDA) ordered 23andMe, a genetic testing company, to stop providing reports on health conditions to purchasers of saliva collection kits.[17] Cofounded by Anne Wojcicki, wife of Google cofounder Sergey Brin, the company was giving information related to how personal genetic information could affect future health, along with

---

16 McGoldrick et al., 2008.
17 BBC, 2013, para. 11.

ancestry-related profiles. The FDA stated that the company had not submitted adequate proof about the accuracy of its detection methods with regard to health conditions. There was further discussion of the appropriateness of providing medical information out of the context of a medical setting.

In 2017, after submitting reports on the consistency and reliability of their tests, 23andMe was given the green light to provide diagnostic risk results for several conditions: late-onset Alzheimer's disease, Parkinson's disease, celiac disease, hereditary thrombophilia, alpha-1 antitrypsin deficiency, glucose-6-phosphate dehydrogenase deficiency, early-onset of dystonia, factor XI deficiency, and Gaucher's disease.[18] In 2019, colorectal cancer was added to this list.[19]

The availability of genetic tests offering risk information regarding one's predisposition to diseases offers advantages and disadvantages. On one hand, people who are informed about their risks could take proactive measures to adopt healthier behaviors; on the other, risks do not mean one will get the disease and could lead to patients who rely on such tests "to self-manage their treatment through dose changes or even abandon certain therapies depending on the outcome of the assessment."[20] The existence of this data together with direct-to-consumer DNA information also raises questions about racial profiling in health, reminiscent of eugenics. Will insurance companies begin charging more for certain races or ethnicities? Will companies use the information to decide who to hire or fire? Certainly, there are ethical considerations in bundling individual ancestry and health risk information together.

One epidemiologist makes a point that interethnic group comparisons, such as conclusions regarding disease variations among groups of people, raise suspicions of racist agendas. Yet, she emphasizes that health researchers do a disservice when they totally disregard differences, because they are important in informing health care interventions:

> Treatments may need to be tailored, by dose, type, and intervention threshold, to a particular ethnic group.

---

18 Kolata, 2017.
19 Brown, 2019.
20 BBC, 2013, para. 11.

Just as we should not refuse to study socioeconomic differences in disease, simply because socioeconomic status is hard to define, and may, if not interpreted with sensitivity, be used as a weapon for victim blaming, so too we should not shy away from studying ethnic variations in disease.[21]

The debate is not centered around whether there are genetic differences in health disease risks among different racial or ethnic groups; rather, it is how the information is used to provide health care without placing value on one group over another. Another aspect of the debate involves why racial disparities exist. Other variables might interact with genetics to increase or decrease risk, such as environmental, social, and institutional factors. Many factors that are not fixed at birth (for example, ethnicity) are more related to factors such as exposure to environmental toxins, occupation, geographic location, dietary intake, access to medical care, and social class, which need to be considered alongside genetic data to create a complete holistic assessment of disease risk and possible interventions.[22] Indeed, certain health conditions could have a higher prevalence in particular groups because of external factors unrelated to genes. The difficulty in parsing out the effect of each variable makes it difficult to understand why some conditions are more common in one group versus another.

Some statistics showing risks for disorders have been established by researchers. These could be caused by genetic mutations that show up more frequently in particular groups, or by **external variables**. African Americans, for example, have higher rates of sickle cell anemia, cardiovascular disease, diabetes, and certain types of cancer.[23] Tay-Sachs disease is more likely to be found among Ashkenazi Jews and people of French Canadian ancestry.[24] Lactose intolerance is found in about 25% Europeans, 50–80% Hispanic, Black, and Ashkenazi Jews, and almost 100% Asians and American Indians.[25] African and Latin American women have higher

---

21 Chaturvedi, 2001.
22 Risch et al., 2002.
23 Mandal et al., 2015.
24 U.S. National Library of Medicine, n.d.
25 Bhatnagara & Aggarwal, 2007.

incidences of BRCA1/2 mutations linked to breast cancer compared to women of Western European ancestry; Ashkenazi Jews also have high incidence rates of BRCA1/2 mutations.[26] Cystic fibrosis occurs more in Whites than non-Whites.[27] It was found that "the prevalence of obesity was lower among non-Hispanic Asian adults (12.7%) compared with all other race and Hispanic-origin groups. Hispanic (47.0%) and non-Hispanic Black (46.8%) adults had a higher prevalence of obesity than non-Hispanic White adults (37.9%)."[28] The incidence of cardiovascular disease is higher among Blacks and American Indians, and Blacks, Mexican Americans, and American Indians have a higher prevalence of diabetes than Whites.[29]

Awareness of Diseases and Health-Seeking Behavior

As communication scholars, we were interested in variables related to people's awareness of diseases that might be more common for their specific ethnicities, and health-seeking behaviors related to their care. For example, do participants associate certain health conditions with their race? To what do they attribute causes? Where do participants go to seek information about health conditions? Knowing this could assist health promotion campaigns in targeting interventions for at-risk populations. In one iteration of the DNA Discussion Project, we asked participants whether they thought there was a link between race/ethnicity and health conditions. Out of 1,527 respondents, 69% stated they believed links existed, and another 27% said they were not sure. The percentages were fairly constant among different ancestry groupings, ranging from 65–73% for those who mentioned having White, Asian, Black, Latinx, and Indigenous in their self-identification. We then sought to find out if those individuals who said yes could identify what diseases they associated with their race/ethnic background to see if awareness matched the literature on genetic predispositions for specific conditions.

---

26 Hall et al., 2009.
27 Schrijver et al., 2015.
28 Hales et al., 2017.
29 American Heart Association, 2011.

Overall, respondents' knowledge matched prevalence statistics for cardiovascular disease, diabetes, lactose intolerance, obesity, sickle cell anemia, and Tay-Sachs disease. Knowledge of BRCA and cystic fibrosis did not match data on prevalence for specific groups.

We looked at how many people sought information regarding their genetic predisposition to health conditions and found that only 15% did so. Among those who did so, half went to health professionals, 33% relied on family and friends, and 29% looked online; 6% used media (including print brochures and mass media), and almost no one said they went to their insurance companies (see Table 7.1). When we looked at racial/ethnic groupings, an interesting story emerged. Whites relied more on health professionals compared to non-Whites, while non-Whites went primarily to their friends and family (see Table 7.2) Our information shows a

TABLE 7.1 Where Respondents Sought Information Regarding Their Genetic Predisposition to Health Conditions

Sought information from (n = 227)	
Health professional	50.7
Family and friends	33.0
Online/internet	29.1
Media, including print brochures and mass media	6.2
Insurance	0.1

TABLE 7.2 Racial/Ethnic Breakdown of Health-Seeking Behavior

	White (n = 174)	Black (n = 48)	Asian (n = 6)	Latinx (n = 13)	Indigenous (n = 8)
Health professional	56.9	37.5	16.7	15.4	25.0
Family/friends	29.9	39.6	50.0	61.5	25.0
Online/internet	27.0	35.4	16.7	38.5	62.5
Media	6.9	4.2	0.0	7.7	0.0

great deal of room for improving health knowledge in society, and our data give us interesting information on ways to begin. More knowledge about health risks and predispositions toward illnesses can support everything from healthier living to compliance in taking medications to greater trust in health providers.

There are ongoing studies to correlate genetic and environmental information with psychiatric and addiction disorders, although many have been hard to replicate and are therefore by no means definitive.[30] Previous research on psychiatric genetics has frequently lacked representation from certain ethnic and age groups. Different groups may have divergent levels of understanding in terms of genetic associations with psychiatric phenotypes.

The story of health and genetics is a complicated one, and we are in the earliest stages of exploring the possibilities and implications. It would be untrue to say that a genetic profile can tell us everything we need to know about health status and its links to ancestry. It is also true that what we have learned so far has been remarkable, and the future will bring additional insights. The DNA Discussion Project is involved in a study with other research institutions to help better understand the relationship between genetics and certain predispositions. Overall, the totality of research holds the potential to improve our health but, of course, must be approached with care and caution.

DISCUSSION QUESTIONS

1. What intersection in your life (race, age, gender, ability etc.) makes your experience unique and different than what people might imagine?

2. How far back can you go in identifying your family ancestors?

3. Might something that happened four generations back shape your life and outlook now?

4. Whatever your background, is there some historical event that shapes how you experience your culture?

---

30 Barnett & Smoller, 2009; Clarke et al., 2017; Ionnidis, 2005; Kendler et al., 2003; Merikangas et al., 1998.

5. Discuss the health narrative of your family. Do people talk about health predispositions because of your race or ethnicity?

ACTIVITIES

1. Create a class panel of volunteers who are willing to talk about a topic, like gender, across different ethnicities.

2. Using the notations included on Figure 7.3 in this chapter, develop your own genogram and see if you can imagine gaining insight using this as an instrument to spark discussion in any context.

LEARN MORE

What Does Our DNA Tell Us

Web Link: https://tinyurl.com/y2axhzyw

CREDITS

Fig. 7.1: Adapted from Maria Dominguez, https://goqnotes.com/48367/intersectionality-and-assemblage-a-real-life-definition/. Copyright © 2016 by Qnotes.

Fig. 7.2: Copyright © 2019 Depositphotos/dmbaker.

Fig. 7.3: Edraw, "Genogram," https://www.edrawsoft.com/en/genogram/genogram-symbols.html. Copyright © by Edrawsoft.

8

ETHICS AND GENETICS

Is My DNA Me or Mine?

Privacy concerns are at the top of the list when people have objections to direct-to-consumer DNA testing. Let's explore the genesis of such concerns, asking Why worry? and Where are we today?

Why Worry?
Historical Breaches of Trust

Henrietta Lacks was diagnosed with a lethal form of cervical cancer in 1951. It is believed that her cancer was caused by the HPV virus,[1] for which there is a vaccine today. If you have received the HPV, polio, or other vaccination, or received treatment for cancer of any kind, or benefitted from some of the most important research in medicine, you can probably thank Henrietta Lacks.[2] Thank you, Henrietta Lacks.

The basis for Ms. Lacks's contribution was the unique nature of her cancer cells. Up until the cultivation of HeLa cells, scientists had not had much luck in sustaining living cells outside of the human body. But HeLa cells were different; these cells lived and lived and allowed scientists to study elements of cell biology formerly not possible. HeLa cells changed science. Yet, Henrietta Lacks, a poor Black woman from Baltimore, died so impoverished

---

1   Kaylin, 2006.
2   Skloot, 2010.

that her family could not afford a headstone for her grave. Many of her family members could not even afford health insurance.[3]

As we talk about the amassing of DNA data from the millions of saliva samples voluntarily given to direct-to-consumer DNA labs, some of the same questions from decades ago give pause to people considering taking the tests. In our experience, the number-one objection people have to taking a direct-to-consumer DNA test has to do with privacy and proprietorship of their data. Their concern is often expressed as, "How do I know what they will do with my DNA?"

Drilling down, people ask what insurance companies will do if they learn about preexisting conditions, if law enforcement will find them or their relatives using their DNA, or how pharmaceutical companies might access and use their data. One person considering participation said specifically, "Suppose there is something special about my DNA? Somebody else gets rich and I get nothing." Definitely shadows of Henrietta Lacks (see Figure 8.1).

Figure 8.1 Henrietta Lacks historical marker.

---

3   Ibid.

A more recent and lesser-known account is shared by genetics writer Priscilla Wald. She reports, "In 1984 the Hagahai people of Papua New Guinea requested medical assistance for the many diseases that were afflicting them. An anthropologist who made contact with the group took blood samples for diagnostic purposes, but when medical researchers discovered unusual immunological properties in the blood of many Hagahai, they used the samples for research and even patented a cell line derived from the DNA of one man."[4]

Another case relates to the Havasupai Tribe of people living in the Grand Canyon region. This case, while relatively unknown, highlights many of the concerns people have regarding usage of direct-to-consumer DNA data. In 1989, researchers from Arizona State University (ASU) embarked on an ultimately unsuccessful research project to try to address high rates of type II diabetes among the Havasupai Tribe. The university then, without permission, used the samples containing DNA for other unrelated studies such as studies on schizophrenia, migration, and inbreeding, all of which are taboo topics for the Havasupai. The tribe discovered the misuse inadvertently when one of their members attended a lecture at ASU.[5]

The National Congress of American Indians reports that in 2004 the Havasupai Tribe filed a lawsuit against Arizona Board of Regents and ASU researchers for misuse of their DNA samples.[6] They state, "These actions have violated the Havasupai Tribe's and tribal members' cultural, religious, and legal rights and have caused the Havasupai Tribe and its members severe emotional distress."[7] Eventually, the *Arizona Board of Regents v. Havasupai Tribe* case reached a settlement in April 2010.

Further, the National Congress of American Indians states their concern about using DNA samples for genetic migration studies. Their worry is that, if a migration study suggests that a tribe originally came across the Bering Strait from Asia, the results of

---

4   Wald, 2008, p. 19.
5   National Congress of the American Indian & American Indiana and
    Alaska Native Genetics Resource Center, n.d.
6   Ibid.
7   FindLaw, n.d.

the study might have political implications and challenge tribal sovereignty and land rights.

Finally, there are concerns that an element of the Havasupai Tribe research relates to "inbreeding." The term is misleading, because any relatively small group with an ethnic identification tends to procreate within its own cultural collective. Because the Havasupai Tribe is small, the inbreeding coefficient assigned to them by researchers was relatively high. For obvious reasons tribal members worried about the stigma associated with such a label both within and beyond their own community.

Where Are We Today?

We'd like to hope that we are advancing in knowledge and sensitivity about informed consent and ethics regarding the millions of DNA samples now in existence. Today, new direct-to-consumer DNA techniques brush up against entities like insurance companies, law enforcement, and big data pharmaceuticals. User concerns touch on fields of education as diverse as actuarial sciences, criminal justice, business, and health. The implications of the growing DNA database are yet to be fully recognized. Many of the possibilities are positive but should be thoughtfully considered as part of any discussion of who we are, the reach of our selfhood, and the extent to which our most intimate data can be extracted and shared, used and exploited, for the common good or for profit.

To some extent the question is "To what degree do we 'own' our genetic identity?" We may ask, "To what extent is my DNA me or mine?" Next, in this chapter we briefly consider some of the issues that arise in the case examples presented and beyond. Obviously, we will not be able to discuss these subjects in great detail; however, the goal throughout this book is to begin a conversation. In that spirit, we address four important questions here: (a) When I give my saliva sample, what am I giving up? (b) Will my privacy be invaded, especially by law enforcement? (c) Could my health care or employment be compromised? and (d) Who should benefit: society, pharmaceutical companies, me?

What Am I Giving Up?

Direct-to-consumer DNA companies want your business, so they are motivated to protect their public images, and that is done by being responsive to public concerns. Any credible company will have a published privacy statement. The largest companies do actually take pains to post readable versions of their policies.[8] If you plan to take a direct-to-consumer DNA test, take the time to look at the statement. The important information is there, but many people just do not read it.[9]

Once you send in your saliva sample and register your kit, you become part of that company's customer base. These companies may use cookies to track you to provide more responsive services. And they do gather public data about you from the internet (e.g., through individual accounts from platforms such as Twitter).

When you register a kit, you may be asked to give permission for your data to be used in research. You may be asked to complete follow-up surveys as part of that research. If you give this permission, you may be recruited to participate in other research outside of the original direct-to-consumer DNA company. DNA companies also may partner with other entities, including pharmaceuticals. There is no commitment from any companies we know of to tell you or compensate you if they find something "usable" in your DNA. And some companies do look for such qualities. This may feel frustrating for some, but on a positive note, your DNA could help lead to important medical insights that could benefit you and society at large.

In general, in terms of your rights, you can ask for your individual information to be deleted, or you can withdraw permission to be involved in research or from the company altogether. If you have consented to have your sample used for research that will continue until you proactively opt out by contacting the company. But remember, if your data is already part of research or has been shared, it may not be completely retrievable. Data on health, **migration patterns**, and so on may have been used in the aggregate and cannot be withdrawn. Some companies automatically keep your

---

8   23andMe, 2020; Ancestry, n.d.b.; Family Search, 2018; MyHeritage, 2020.
9   Molteni, 2018a.

DNA indefinitely; others give you the option for how your sample will be managed. Again, read the posted information.

Finally, remember that if you download your raw data from a direct-to-consumer DNA site and then upload it to a public site, like GEDMatch, you have made your own data public, and it can be accessed and used without your specific permission. Know that outsiders can and do scan these sites.[10]

One such case was covered in the news. The notorious Golden Gate killer was arrested in part based on the use of open DNA sources. The Golden Gate killer, also known as the East Side Rapist, the Visalia Ransacker, and the Original Night Stalker, committed crimes between 1974 and 1986. He avoided detection for decades but was identified in 2018 based on DNA data of his distant relatives submitted to a public site. The killer was identified as Joseph James DeAngelo. And now he stands accused of 50 rapes and 12 murders.[11] In other cases, citizen investigators have used these sites to locate missing victims and solve other mysteries.[12] Also, be aware that virtually all of the DNA companies will and must comply with a valid search warrant from law enforcement.[13]

Will My Privacy Be Invaded By Law Enforcement?

Even a casual fan of law and order television knows that the police generally need a search warrant to invade your privacy as an American citizen; to enter and search your home or car, even your cell phone content. But how about your DNA profile?

If compelled, companies will provide data to law enforcement.[14] Most will resist to some extent, however. More recent technology has nothing to do with ancestry profiles and relates to the ability of law enforcement (or others) to obtain a DNA sample from an individual from a crime scene and build a physical likeness of the person as a police drawing, which may be just as helpful as a

---

10 Molteni, 2018b.
11 Molteni, 2019.
12 DNA Doe Project, n.d.
13 23andMe, 2020; Ancestry, n.d.b.; MyHeritage, 2020.
14 23andMe, n.d.

DNA search. Technology marches forward. In other words, access to you via your DNA has become even easier than compelling a direct-to-consumer DNA company to turn over data. Using ancestry profiles is often a more indirect and more difficult way to identify you. Direct-to-consumer companies do not want to be placed in this position to have to give up their data, and, as noted, they have resisted it,[15] so this is not the road of least resistance for law enforcement. The 23andMe post related to law enforcement reads, "23andMe chooses to use all practical legal and administrative resources to resist requests from law enforcement, and we do not share customer data with any public databases, or with entities that may increase the risk of law enforcement access. In certain circumstances, however, 23andMe may be required by law to comply with a valid court order, subpoena, or search warrant for genetic or personal information."[16]

In cases where genetic data *is* mined, we can consider when this data can be of social value. Citizen sleuths Margaret Press and Colleen Fitzpatrick in their DNA Doe Project[17] assist individuals and law enforcement in finding serial killers and locating and identifying the missing. Another instance is The Innocence Project, founded by attorneys Peter Neufeld and Barry Scheck, that has exonerated more than 365 people in the United States using DNA testing, including 20 people who served time on death row.[18]

Beyond law enforcement, direct-to-consumer DNA companies we reviewed do not provide information to insurance companies or employers.

Could My Health Care or Employment Be Compromised?

The federal Genetic Information Nondiscrimination Act (GINA) explicitly prohibits health insurers and employers from considering genetic information when providing coverage. Passed in 2008, GINA prohibits "discrimination on the basis of genetic information

---

15 Ibid.
16 Ibid., para. 8.
17 DNA Doe Project, n.d.
18 The Innocence Project, n.d.

with respect to health insurance and employment."[19] At the state level, according to the ACLU, "Twenty-four states have enacted laws that either provide protection against genetic discrimination or which prohibit genetic testing in either the insurance or employment setting."[20] According to Moody's Corporation, a major risk management agency, currently, many state laws "restrict life insurers from using genetic information in their underwriting process, and life insurers currently do not explicitly ask individuals for their genetic information."[21] In general, genetic results are treated as a form of private property. Moody's has responded with reserve but later accepted the limitations of the uses of genetic data in providing coverage. Pragmatic, as expected, they state, "For health and life insurers, genetic testing technology could lead to cost-effective treatments, a positive for both industries. Prolonging life spans would be a positive for life insurers that are responsible for paying large amounts of death benefits, because they would collect and invest premiums on in-force policies longer than anticipated."[22] You are a better deal to life insurance companies if you live longer!

Notably, many socially conscious people who have shared their DNA data feel that the answer to insurance and health concerns is not privacy legislation at all, but rather broad sweeping measures to limit the negative outcomes of breaches of privacy.[23] Many of these people express that in the age of ubiquitous genetic testing as well as mass and social media, privacy as we knew it is already a thing of the past. Rather, they argue, we should ensure against the vulnerabilities of some by guaranteeing benefits like universal health care coverage or even a guaranteed minimum income.

Big Pharma: Who Should Benefit?

Some of the most intriguing work in the area of direct-to-consumer DNA relates to pharmaceuticals, and race and ancestry, especially. It was only in 2005 that the drug BiDil was approved specifically

---

19 Equal Employment Opportunity Commission, 2008.
20 American Civil Liberties Union, n.d.
21 Moody Investor's Service, 2018.
22 Ibid., para. 6.
23 Haeusermann et al., 2018.

for use by African Americans. At that time, the *New York Times* hailed it as both "controversial" and a "step toward a new frontier of personalized medicine."[24] Clearly, personalized medicine is the wave of the future. Of course, in the DNA Discussion Project, we found that the definition of "African American" as well as other racial/ethnic categories have often been vague and contested. A genetic neurobiologist friend refers to common racial categories as little more than folklore. This blunt terminology is surely less than ideal in targeting medication and can be detrimental in some cases if prescribed incorrectly. Today, the idea of precision medicine has become much more sophisticated, and research on genomics is a critical underpinning. Establishing large data pools is key.

To this end, Kubick states that "we need to pool diverse sources and types of data together" to "build much more understanding of the genetic profiles of patients and seek out genetic markers that may predict their response to various types of drugs to inform the physician's treatment plan with predictive evidence."[25] It should not be a surprise to anyone that direct-to-consumer DNA companies are involved in this work. With samples in the millions, these companies are an alluring target for any pharmaceutical research agency. In fact, some of the world's biggest drug makers are gaining exclusive rights to data from direct-to-consumer DNA companies.[26] In the shadows of Henrietta Lacks, companies are seeking access to large data sets to find people with unusual mutations that can point to targets for new drugs. Science writer Sarah Zhang reports that "the best example of this is a gene called PCSK9, which scientists in Texas found by chance when studying people with unusually high and unusually low cholesterol."[27] The *PCSK9* gene provides instructions for making a protein that helps regulate the amount of cholesterol in the bloodstream.[28] Popular drugs Repatha and Praluent, a class of cholesterol-lowering drugs called "PCSK9 inhibitors," are based on this science. There is also research on other genetic variations like resistance to HIV.[29]

---

24 Saul, 2005.
25 Kubick, 2013.
26 Molteni, 2018a.
27 Zhang, 2018.
28 Ingelsson & Knowles, 2017.
29 Tebas et al., 2014.

Some direct-to-consumer DNA companies have been commod-
ifying health and genetic data for years, with mixed experience.
Forbes magazine reported in 2003 that the Food and Drug Administration had chastised 23andMe for acting as a drug company and
giving health information to customers while presenting itself as
a fun way to learn about personal science:

> 23andMe's business was never going to be selling genetic
> test kits at $100 a pop; even if the company reaches its
> goal of selling 1 million kits cumulatively, that's only
> $100 million in revenue, a small sum by the standards
> of biotech and play money at Google [an investor].
> But what a large enough database of people who were
> sharing not only genetic information but information
> about their health and their bodies offered was some-
> thing greater: a tool that could be used to find new
> genetic connections, for detecting drug side effects,
> maybe even for finding new diagnostics or cures. That's
> why 23andMe needs to get to 1 million kits sold—to
> build that database. That promise has brought on other
> investors, including Facebook billionaire Yuri Milner.
>
> If the selling point of the 23andMe kit was that it
> allowed people to participate in science, maybe the FDA
> could have let this go. But 23andMe's website specifically
> told the story of people who got test results related to
> breast cancer genes. The FDA probably felt it had little
> choice. This is not the story of a big regulator choos-
> ing to squash a small company, but of a company that
> decided that it didn't have to follow the rules.[30]

The fear of being exploited or mistreated in any number of ways
based on our personal DNA data is understandable. Our genetic
profile is an extension of our very self, and being probed or com-
modified for it has a feeling of taint to it. But there are also risks
in not moving forward vigorously in this work. It is advancements
in science that have moved the average life expectancy from age
47 at the turn of the 1900 to 78 in 2007.[31] It is, to some degree,

---

30 Herper, 2013.
31 Centers for Disease Control and Prevention, 2010.

fear and resentment of pharmaceuticals that has led some people to avoid vaccination and to reject medical intervention and leave an opening for the return of diseases once thought to be almost eradicated.[32] No doubt, we should always question the motivation of anyone with a profit (or even research) incentive, but we should not ignore the opportunities for good outcomes for insurers, law enforcement, or pharma to improve the lives of everyone. For sure, more advancements are in store, as well as challenges.

In contrast to people who fear being exploited by the legal-medical establishment, there are people who feel that it is the social responsibility of individuals to make their DNA profiles available for research that may benefit society,[33] especially those who are less vulnerable in terms of losing medical coverage or being otherwise harmed by exposure. These people are not necessarily thinking of for-profit organizations, and, of course, the pharmaceutical industry and direct-to-consumer DNA companies are for profit. So, a question for direct-to-consumer DNA test takers may be, what are the costs and benefits to individuals, like ourselves, to allow what we initially sought out as a test for a simple ancestry profile to now be used for far-reaching purposes and profit?

The idea that some people are more vulnerable (and suspicious) than others was highlighted on a West Chester University panel about the book *The Immortal Life of Henrietta Lacks,* whose life story is highlighted in Chapter 7. The panel was hosted by the DNA Discussion Project and the Minorities in Medicine student club at West Chester University. This student organization has the goal of supporting undergraduates interested in medical fields and also exploring health issues of special interest to minority people. For the *Lacks* panel, these students of color shared their own backgrounds and ancestry profiles and talked about their experience with the medical establishment. Many of their stories were very negative. They included instances of being disregarded or receiving inferior treatment. The majority of the students felt that the Lacks family was exploited. In discussion, many commented on other infamous cases of Black and poor people being misused in medicine; the Tuskegee Syphilis Study and the *Buck v. Bell* sterilization

---

32 Felter, 2019.
33 Haeusermann et al., 2018.

case, for example, were mentioned. Of course, these studies would not pass research oversight standards today.

The Tuskegee Syphilis Study and the *Buck v. Bell*[34] U.S. Supreme Court case are two pivotal examples of exploitation and mistreatment of the vulnerable in society. In his book *Bad Blood: The Tuskegee Syphilis Experiment,* James Jones reports that "in late July 1972, Jean Heller of the Associated Press broke the story: for forty years the United States Public Health Service (PHS) had been conducting a study of the effects of untreated syphilis on black men in Macon County, Alabama"[35] He reports that there never was a formal protocol. Meanwhile, 400 mostly poor Black men and their spouses and children were allowed to suffer and die of the disease untreated, simply so that data could be collected up to their deaths from syphilis and related conditions. No new drugs were tested and the efficacy of current treatments never explored. The case became a profile of unethical medical exposure. In the *Buck v. Bell* case (which is presented in greater detail in Chapter 9 of this book) a poor White woman was forced into sterilization, a decision upheld by the U.S. Supreme Court because she was determined to be a legal "moron." Such cases are chilling in our history. Of course, health care disparities based on race and social class exist today and are forward in the minds of students like those participating on the *Lacks* panel.

Notably on this panel was one dissenting voice. This individual was a professor who had worked all his life in the medical field. He was an older, nonminority gentleman. He stated dispassionately that Ms. Lacks's treatment was in keeping with the treatment of the times, that the individual scientists who took her cell sample did not become wealthy, and that her cells benefited society, including, undoubtedly, some of the very students participating on the panel. In fact, he added, many people of color worked on Henrietta Lacks's cells as laboratory technicians and were an important part of the work in discovery. There are no simple answers.

Today, saliva samples of over 12 million people taking direct-to-consumer DNA tests make up a potential treasure trove for scientific research, no doubt. What attitudes do you carry from your past that shape your attitudes about research today? What

---

34 *Buck v. Bell*, 1927.
35 Jones, 1993, p. 276.

are *you* willing to share about your genome? Today, we are faced with legal and moral questions unique to our times. Every decision has its benefits and drawbacks. Only through open and educated discussion can we even begin to work through the complexities to benefit ourselves and society.

Who are we? We are unique individuals genetically and culturally. And yet, our very genome links us, and unlocking the secrets of that genome has consequences for us all. That makes our futures inextricably linked.

DISCUSSION QUESTIONS

1. Should we be paid for information gleaned from our DNA?

2. Are there limits to how and how much our DNA data should be our private possession? How about letting others see our genes for research?

3. How often have you agreed to an online contract by mindlessly clicking "agree"? Whose responsibility is that? With so many contracts in our lives today, how are you and the public at large protected?

4. Overall, do you think more good or bad comes from the use of DNA data by law enforcement? How does your experience with law enforcement shape your perception?

5. Do you think our race, gender, social class, and health status shape our attitudes about issues of privacy and sharing genetic material? What are the implications of this?

ACTIVITIES

1. Select someone you know, but not well. Just looking at this person's public data, identify 10 facts that you can learn about this person. Should this worry or surprise us?

2. Identify some conditions that you associate with your ethnic group. Conduct research to determine if your belief is supported. What other conditions can you find? What treatments are available?

LEARN MORE

Race Underneath the Skin

Web Link: https://tinyurl.com/y4md79l4

9

WHAT'S NEW

What Is on the Horizon in Direct-to-Consumer DNA Testing?

Clearly, we are on the verge of even more new and complicated options based on the easy availability of genetic data, particularly related to ancestry, but also relating to sex, ability, and social class. Understanding what genes can and cannot say about who we are and can be is key in this conversation. In this chapter, we look at what's in the news to see what people are talking about and preparing for, asking, "What's on the horizon?" The first theme is genetically enhancing babies often referred to as "designer babies," which, it turns out, is not so new. Second, we look at the growth of precision medicine and the objective of making treatment more and more individually targeted, sometimes related to ancestry. We discuss the dangers in attempting to predict who is worthy and the eugenics movement, which had benevolent motives, gone awry. We mention one concern that has been raised about biowarfare based on genetic distinctiveness. We reinforce the idea that racial animus did not require direct-to-consumer DNA testing to be in full force. Third, we mention the new and growing area of epigenetics, which makes the case that genetics at birth are not the entire picture. The impact of environmental factors on any individual's growth and development can be significant. Finally, we end by presenting new developments in the DNA Discussion Project.

The Best Babies?!

Lulu and Nana's exact birthday is unknown, but their arrival was announced on November 25, 2018, via YouTube by Chinese researcher Jian-kui He. According to He, his team had "created" the world's first genetically altered human babies. Specifically, the team used the CRISPR-Cas9 (Clustered Regularly Interspaced Short Palindromic Repeat) genome-editing tool to disable a gene involved in helping HIV to enter healthy cells. You will recall that one of the goals of developing genetic medicine is to combat HIV. It was later revealed that the same alteration has been found to improve memory in mice, and there is speculation that that may have been a motivation for the alteration as well.[1]

As you can imagine, the project was met with extreme skepticism. An *Atlantic* magazine article identified 15 specific legal or ethical violations associated with the experiment, among them that the alteration did not meet "an unmet medical need,"[2] the "actual editing wasn't executed well,"[3] "there were problems with informed consent,"[4] and He "acted in contravention of global consensus."[5] Yet, Jian-kui He's work continues today and he has presented the idea of "genetic medical tourism"[6] as a vision for the future. In a survey that He sponsored, the scientist found that 60% of the Chinese population viewed the technology favorably. Some have speculated that this is part of culture wars between the east and west.

Futuristic science fiction lets us directly address related fears from the past. So-called designer babies have been in the news for decades and bring to the fore recollections of the eugenics movement in the United States (referenced several times earlier in this text) that came into prominence in the early 1900s. It was sometimes called the "better babies" movement.[7] The initial goals may have been laudable, to eliminate suffering and improve society, and yet the movement brought about laws in some 19 states that called for the sterilization of the "feebleminded"[8] and others, including those with epilepsy, and often minorities and the poor. The **better baby movement** resulted in the sterilization of over 64,000 people across 30 U.S. states.

---

1   Regalado, 2019.
2   Yong, 2018, para. 4.
3   Ibid., para. 6.
4   Ibid., para. 11.
5   Ibid., para. 20.
6   Cohen, 2019.
7   Oveyssi, 2015.
8   Debunking Denial, n.d.

In the 1927 landmark Supreme Court decision *Buck v. Bell*, the court supported the right to sterilize inmates in institutions, like asylums. The case centered around Carrie Buck, a poor White woman whose mother and grandmother had both been identified as intellectually disabled. Many have challenged this categorization. In elementary school Carrie did average work until she was removed from school by her foster parents so that she could help with housekeeping in their home. Carrie was raped by her foster parents' nephew and she became pregnant. The foster parents then had her committed to an institution. Carrie wanted to keep her baby, but in 1924 she gave birth to a daughter who was taken from her because she was deemed incompetent and promiscuous. Custody was given to the foster family whose nephew had raped her. The institution petitioned to have Carrie sterilized under Virginia law and the case was a test case in the U.S. Supreme Court, with Carrie having no real representation. In 1927 the court ruled against Carrie Buck, forcing her to be sterilized. In a well-known decision, Supreme Court Justice Oliver Wendell Holmes stated, "Three generations of imbeciles is enough."[9] Carrie was sterilized later that year. Her 13-year-old sister was also sterilized without her knowledge or consent. Both sisters married in their lifetimes. Both regretted not being able to have children. Before she died of a childhood ailment, the child taken away from Carrie Buck was on the honor roll at school.[10]

The eugenics movement began to wane in the 1940s, generally in response to the eugenic horrors committed against Jews in Nazi Germany. The idea that certain classes of people are undesirable based on supposed genetic limitations of disability or ethnicity or race was seen as antithetical to American values but have existed since before genetic testing of any kind was possible, as in the case of Carrie Buck. *Buck v. Bell* was never overturned. The last forced sterilizations occurred into the 1970s. However, in a report on National Public Radio about the *Buck v. Bell* case, it is reported that

> while campaigns of mass sterilization are in our past, the ideas that inspired those campaigns live on. Dozens of women were sterilized without their consent in the

---

9   *Buck v. Bell*, 1927.
10   Lombardo, 2008.

California prison system between 2005 and 2011. In 2017, a judge in Tennessee offered reduced jail time to inmates who agreed to be sterilized in order to … "break a vicious cycle of repeat drug offenders with children." The eugenicists were utopians convinced that they were doing hard but necessary things. As much as we might like to relegate their actions to the history books, it's important to pay attention, to make sure we are not carrying their ideas with us in a new edition, freshly-bound, shining with the possibility of a brighter future.[11]

Anyone who has a rags-to-riches story in their family or who is a part of a once (or currently) demonized group should be wary of those who posit that genetic information can predict who should be allowed to procreate. Genetics can help us improve our lives, cure disease, and make a better society. Along the way, we must avoid the arrogance that suggests that the vulnerable are of no value and should be denied self-determination.

By the 1970s a new baby controversy was erupting. This time the rage was about "**test tube babies**." These were female eggs fertilized outside of the uterus and then implanted into the mother. While in the early days there were criticisms of the process being unnatural, today, more than six million children have been conceived via "in vitro fertilization" with very little notice.

DNA testing *has* brought some of these cases to the fore, however. One woman known to the DNA Discussion Project took a test and found not only her ancestry, but that she had more than 29 half siblings—and those were only the ones who took the same direct-to-consumer DNA test she took! Apparently, the fertilization lab had used one donor multiple times.

Beyond isolated scandals (and they are important to consider), **in vitro fertilization** and **genetic profiling** create the possibility of selecting the "best" zygote for implantation. The definition of "best," as you can imagine, opens the door for "an ethical morass."[12] In 2009, the magazine *Scientific American* opened the article "The Need to Regulate 'Designer Babies'" saying

---

11 Schmidt, 2018.
12 Joseph, 2017.

On March 3 the cover story of the *New York Daily News* trumpeted a simple imperative to "Design Your Baby." The screaming headline related to a service that would try to allow parents to choose their baby's hair, eye and skin color. A day later the Fertility Institutes [the authors of the ad] reconsidered. The organization made an "internal, self-regulatory decision" to scrap the project because of "public perception" and the "apparent negative societal impacts involved," it noted in a statement.[13]

Hmm, choose your "baby's hair, eye, and skin color"? Sounds a lot like race selection. Indeed, some of these are the very genetic markers that are deemed "ancestry informative" and are associated with what we commonly refer to as a person's race. The Fertility Institutes is still building the foundation for a nascent dial-a-trait catalogue, and it routinely accepts clients who wish to select the sex of their child.

It is noteworthy that hair, eye, and skin color are all associated with ethnicity. Is the possibility of selecting the hair, eyes, skin color, and sex of a child a bad or good thing? Would giving people the opportunity to get the baby "they want" improve parents' ability to nurture the child? Will it give the children a better opportunity for success?

Much was made of Princeton graduate Susan Patton for her book *Marry Smart* when she suggested that young women should find a husband while at elite schools, basically because they are provided with a great gene pool. Does the possibility of enhancing babies reflect the same impulse? Do the "best schools" have the best gene pools?

Of course, many argue that it is not the characteristic of the baby, but the preferences and prejudices of society that disadvantage a child based on color or gender or variants in ability. Is our time better spent educating society rather than narrowing biodiversity? What are the limits of what parents and their doctors should do to "enhance" a child? Should we permit enhancements to change color? How about size and shape, height, deafness, ADD, schizophrenia? Are we assuming that certain undesirable characteristics

---

13 *Scientific American*, 2009, para. 1.

will be detrimental in the future? Might we have eliminated people with poor vision before the invention of eyeglasses? Might people who seem different or disabled today be enabled tomorrow? Do people who are different provide unique advantages? What qualities make life and society better?

Along with questions regarding the overall idea of baby enhancing, concerns have been expressed that the wealthy will have access to these choices, further disadvantaging poor people and communities. This problem is not new, of course. The wealthy have always had greater access to enhanced prenatal and pediatric health care, education and housing, and social networks. What should be the limits, if any?

Other controversial birth-related technologies have included birth control or abortion, which have been suggested as a means of eliminating various groups. Birth control is now estimated to be used in the United States by 98% of sexually active women at some point in their lives. These strategies have been criticized for use in sex selection and weeding out people with disabilities.

Ultimately, each generation and individuals are faced with special challenges, and each has to grapple with the right balance of progress and restraint, personal choice, and social good. Just as in the past, this next generation will have to develop guidelines, laws, and precedents to direct the use of baby-related technology.[14]

The Best Treatment for Me?

In an open access article published in a journal with the goal of providing global visibility on issues of genetics, the authors tell us that there has been a "recent and unremarked upon emergence of biomedical studies linking markers of genetic ancestry to disease risks."[15] They share that this body of scientific research has become part of public discourse and is connecting ancestry and health in the public mind. They warn "that the boundary between ancestry-related and health-related genetic testing is more porous than previously suggested."[16] Further, they assert that the decreas-

---

14 Bouche & Rivard, 2014.
15 Smart et al., 2017, para. 2.
16 Ibid., para. 6.

ing cost of even broader genetic testing will make personal DNA profiles a regular part of health decision making.

Clearly, the future will include genetic tests as an element in personalized medicine. The question is what is the appropriateness? What is the impact? Having easy access to our own genetic data and extensive information on the possible medical implications may change the landscape of medical consultation. There are already multiple websites that people can access to see what gene variants are associated with certain conditions (for example). And there are genetic tests that aim to tell you everything from the best approaches to weight loss to the appropriate anti-depressant for your genetic type.

The National Center for Biotechnology information currently allows individuals to "find genes associated with a phenotype or disease."[17] And they guide people through the process. One website, GeneSight® Psychotropic, touts, "The GeneSight Psychotropic test analyzes how your genes may affect your response to medications commonly prescribed to treat depression. The GeneSight Psychotropic test provides your clinician with information about which medications may require dose adjustments, may be less likely to work for you, or may have an increased risk of side effects based on your genetic makeup."[18] All of this will surely have an impact on the doctor-patient relationship and on what drugs are prescribed and sold, and how various groups link health and background in common thinking. We have already questioned the appropriateness of an individual to independently process the link between genetic information and appropriate health strategies. We have already mentioned that the first personalized drug was targeted toward African Americans. We must step carefully to adequately serve individuals and groups in the future.

The *Business Insider* journal reports on the development of chatbots (robots that you can text or direct message with, similar to normal conversation) and wonders if they might one day play a role in helping deliver the findings of genetic tests. The *Business Insider* reports a spokesperson of Helix Genomics saying, "To me, part of the balance of providing something responsibly and making

17 National Center for Biotechnology Information, n.d.
18 Genesight, 2020.

a safe and quality experience is making sure the information is provided in a really digestible way."[19]

There is great controversy over the extent to which race will and should play a part in precision medicine. Some make the case that linking race and medical conditions is a distraction and an inappropriate and deceptive conflation. The case can be made that "if you want to understand heart failure, you look at heart failure, and if you want to understand racial disparities in conditions such as heart failure or hypertension, there is much to look at that has nothing to do with genetics."[20] Others disagree and feel that not addressing any link in ancestral causation is irresponsible.[21] Ask yourself, would it be important if certain ethnic groups were more susceptible to depression? Does it matter that Asians tend to be lactose intolerant or Ashkenazi Jews have a higher incidence of the BRCA1 gene? How Asian or Jewish does a person have to be to be at higher risk? Does this knowledge cause us to approach Asian health care and Jewish health care in skewed ways? Does it cause us to miss these conditions in individuals in other groups? Would you agree that "the only valid way to understand what is in a person's DNA is to study that individual's DNA"?[22] As direct-to-consumer DNA testing becomes less costly, might it make better sense to just test everyone for everything? Should the federal government hold this mass of information? Would that data be best processed in a traditional medical consultation, in an e-mail, by a bot? What would you prefer? What do you predict?

On the other end of the care and cure spectrum are those who seek to use our genetic uniqueness to cause harm. Military.com reports that one of the top officers "warned against using popular at-home ancestry DNA test kits this week, saying scientific advancements are making biological weapons more tailorable."[23] Other scientists quoted in the same article assure that such technology is complex and difficult and "not the sort of thing someone might cobble together readily in a garage."[24] Still the article, and most in the know in this era say the obvious; treat your genetic data like personal information and be careful how you share it. The BBC recently reported in October

19 Brodwin, 2019.
20 Wolinsky, 2011, para. 4.
21 Ibid.
22 Blell & Hunter, 2019, para. 8.
23 Harkins, 2019.
24 Ibid., para. 19.

of 2018 that the Kremlin related that foreign agents were collecting data samples of different Russian ethnicities, and they suspected the possibility of bio-warfare.[25] Still, today, most of this type of espionage continues to be the stuff of action films. Remember too that thus far, virtually all of the damage, decimation and genocide done by one human to another has nothing to do with targeted genetic weapons.

Epigenetics: Is It How We Play the Hand We're Dealt?

In 1957 the British scientist Conrad Hal Waddington's book *The Strategy of the Genes* presented a metaphor about the relationship between genetic make-up and what eventually is expressed in an organism.[26] To explain, Waddington talks about how rocks roll down a hill following different paths, based on the terrain they encounter. When the rocks are at the top, many paths are possible. All of the things that happen to the rock on the way down then impact its path. These are the epigenetic factors. Factors can include things like the weather or other rocks and divots or water. While rocks may be identical (or not) at the top, they can end up being vastly divergent at the bottom. Further, if you hope to move a rock from one gully at the bottom of the hill over to a parallel one, it is far harder than directing the path from the top at the outset. And one has to question how far back up the hill you have to retrace in order to effectively redirect after the rock has landed. And what herculean interventions have to be made to change a trajectory? This metaphor became known as Waddington's epigenetic landscape and is at the core of this area of thinking. Epigenetics are those external factors that can actually change our destiny and our progeny, and epigenetics is on the cutting edge of genetic thinking (see Figure 9.1).

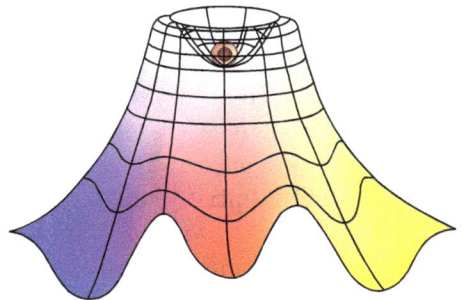

Figure 9.1 Epigenetics concept.

Waddington's work focused on the cellular level, but research has

25 BBC News, 2017.
26 Waddington, 1957.

been conducted on twins and other human organisms in real-world applications. For example, separated and nonseparated identical twins have been followed through life to see what similarities and differences prevail. Babies born at different times during feast and famine have been followed through their life cycles as well.[27]

This emerging research and theory call on us to create the richest environment for every child long before we indulge in theories about inherent ability, especially related to race and gender. It is imperative that we take a sincere look and ask whether we have provided the very optimal setting for every child to maximize that person's potential. If we are honest with ourselves the answer has to be no, whether we look at public school funding based on property taxes (privileging the rich), or the ability of the wealthy to manipulate the system to their advantage or any other advantages of access. The well-circulated college scandal of wealthy parents paying for their children to gain admission into elite schools is but one example.[28] Providing children every chance early in life (at the "top of the hill") can go a long way and can prevent remediation and investments in mass incarceration later in life (at the "bottom of the hill"). Clearly, Waddington's work and his legacy suggests that early work can pay off in great dividends. More research as to how is certainly warranted.

What Is the Future of the DNA Discussion Project?

Ultimately, our curiosity and imagination will define the future. With all of the exciting possibilities ahead, we have enough challenges to keep us going indefinitely.

Moving forward, the DNA Discussion Project is involved in three major initiatives. One project seeks to explore the link between social attitudes and ancestry identity. The second project seeks to explore how we can relate this work across disciplines. Third, we consider if our genetic profiles can give insight to psychological conditions like depression and substance dependency.

---

27 Carey, 2013.
28 Taylor, 2019.

What Is the Link Between Social Attitudes and Ancestry Identity?

The DNA Discussion Project has thus far surveyed more than 3,000 people in research programs. Most of the questions we have raised have been related to general attitudes about how participants see their racial and ethnic identity. We have since moved into questions about awareness of ancestry-associated conditions and health-seeking behaviors. We are now exploring social attitudes related to identity before and after taking a direct-to-consumer DNA test. Questions now include scaled queries about attitudes and behaviors, including agreement with statements like the following:

- An ideal society requires some groups to be on top and others to be on the bottom.

- The kind of person one is can be largely attributed to genetic inheritance.

- A person's race is fixed at birth.

- If you could choose your neighbors, how strong is your preference for White American versus racial minorities?

- Italian, Irish, and Jewish and many other minorities overcame prejudice and worked their way up; new immigrants should do the same.

We examine both variations among different groups and attitudes before and after taking the direct-to-consumer DNA tests. Findings are still in process. What do you think we'll see? What questions would you want to ask?

Arts and Sciences: How Can We Relate This Work Across Disciplines?

As we continue to explore direct-to-consumer DNA, we are looking at new ways to investigate the data. In a collaboration with a photographic artist in his project *Sum of the Some of Us*, Patrick Ibizugbe looks at the profiles of people who have taken direct-to-consumer DNA tests and conducts interviews about their knowledge and interest in their range of ancestors. He conducts research on the attire of these predecessors during various eras. His talented team then creates costumes inspired by this information. This is followed by a professional photo shoot, generally around three ancestral themes. Finally, he post-interviews participants, discussing how it feels to try on a piece of their ancestors' lives. It is an exciting way to link this work across fields from the arts to the sciences and might be especially engaging for young people (see Figures 9.2–9.5)

Can Genetic Profiles Give Insight to Psychological Conditions?

As suggested, risk of developing a psychiatric disorder is affected by both environmental and genetic influences.[29] Results from large genetic studies on schizophrenia have also indicated that analysis of other psychiatric disorders will benefit from further sample collection and analysis.[30] Furthermore, past research on psychiatric genetics has frequently lacked representation from certain ethnic (e.g., African Americans) and age groups (e.g., young adults). These groups may have different genetic associations with

Figure 9.2 Delano Dunn.

---

29 Barnett & Smoller, 2009; Clarke et al., 2017; Kendler et al., 2003; Merikangas et al., 1998.
30 Schizophrenia Working Group of the Psychiatric Genomics Consortium, 2014.

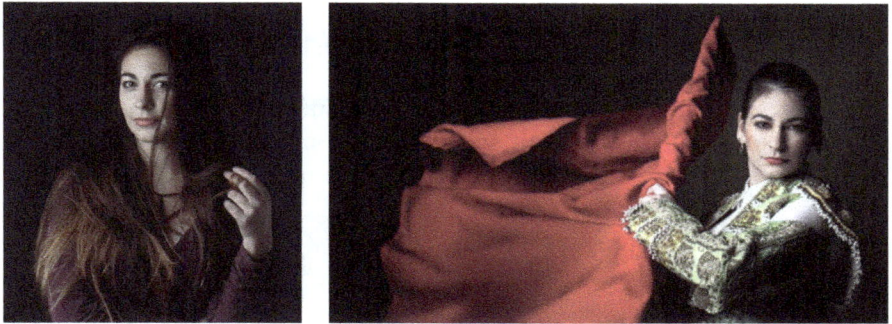

Figure 9.3 Sara Seferian.

Figure 9.4 Anita Foeman.

Figure 9.5 Bessie Lee Lawton.

psychiatric conditions due to differences in genetic background or environmental factors.

Our current project aims to compare the genetically driven results with the individual's prior understanding of their own ancestry. We are asking people who have participated in direct-to-consumer DNA testing to complete a survey, allowing us to look at their gene patterns (anonymously) to see if we determine any relationships.

By completing this project, we will create a valuable resource for psychiatric and addiction genetics research of ethnically diverse and young adult samples that can be used to evaluate genetic associations that are currently unrecognized. This work is of high significance, as developing a deeper understanding of the genetic basis of psychiatric disorders will not only allow us to better predict who will suffer from these disorders but will also allow for genetically informed pharmacological and other treatments to achieve the best patient outcomes.

All in all, our past, current, and future work has allowed us to be a part of an important cultural moment. We feel honored to add our voices and our research to many that are part of this conversation now and ongoing.

We encourage you to engage.

DISCUSSION QUESTIONS

1. What is the difference between a disability and a difference? In a small group, list five qualities that you would place in each category. Does everyone in your group agree?

2. There are ethical commissions who discuss the choices and limitations of genetic manipulation. If you were to design a commission, who would be on it? What would be some of the primary directives?

3. What, if anything, would you do to make genetic advances available to everyone?

4. What qualities would you like your child to have if you are able to manipulate their genes?

5. Can you think of a physical characteristic that is considered a problem today but may not be in the future?

ACTIVITIES

1. Look up websites that allow you to see what your child would look like with a famous person with a different racial background.

2. Create an emoji of yourself but change your characteristics to be what you consider to be ideal. Explain what you changed and why.

LEARN MORE

Professors Using DNA to Bridge Racial Divide, Focus on Our Similarities

Web Link: https://tinyurl.com/y3vfl622

CREDITS

Fig. 9.1: Copyright © by K. T. Rodolfa (cc by 3.0) at https://commons.wikimedia.org/wiki/File:The_epigenetic_landscape_and_its_implications_for_direct_reprogramming..jpg .

Fig. 9.2: Copyright © by Brooklyn McTavish. Reprinted with permission.

Fig. 9.3: Copyright © by Brooklyn McTavish. Reprinted with permission.

Fig. 9.4: Copyright © by Brooklyn McTavish. Reprinted with permission.

Fig. 9.5: Copyright © by Brooklyn McTavish. Reprinted with permission.

ACKNOWLEDGMENTS

I would like to thank so many people who have made this project possible. First, and foremost my parents and brother Lois and Gerald Foeman and Gerald Foeman Jr. who helped me put race in perspective in a difficult era in history. My husband Nate, and kids Chelsea, Nicole, and Darqui and extended family for being so understanding and providing unending support. I am grateful for the community in which I grew up that nurtured me. In my academic life, I thank Terry Nance who is a kindred spirit as well as a mentor. Chris Lynch and Phil Thompsen who carried me professionally at times when it was hard to carry myself. Tina Harris, Gina Bell, and Stacey Peterson who do their own cutting edge work and have supported me as an outlier in so many ways. Maurice Hall, Lisa Huebner, and Martin Remland for their intellectual perceptive in many a situation. I thank my former graduate student assistant and now colleague David Stern. I thank all of my West Chester University colleagues and students. I also want to thank Todd Armstrong and Tony Paese at Cognella for their help in bringing this project to fruition. I thank my wonderful friend and co-author Bessie Lawton. And, of course, more people than I could ever mention here or ever for this wonderful academic life I have led.

—*Anita Foeman*

There are many to thank and not enough space to do so. Thank you to my Papa, Ignacio Lee, who instilled in me the love of travel, which opened my eyes to the rich variety of peoples around the world. To my Mom, Grace Hsieh Lee, who is the ultimate epitome of grace and strength, and showed me creativity is ageless.

I am grateful for Professors at the University of Pennsylvania, Robert Hornik and Oscar Gandy, who had faith in an immigrant from the other side of the world. To West Chester University colleagues and students, and especially the Faculty Senate, where I have grown to feel deeply about campus climate issues and how these affect the education of the students we are serving. Thanks to our editor Todd Armstrong and Tony Paese at Cognella for their patience as we worked to get this project finished.

I remember telling my high school friends that my name will be on a book someday. Thank you to Anita, a wonderful friend, colleague, and mentor, who helped to make this happen. I am grateful for the many years of challenging and eye-opening conversations, ranging from large societal issues to the best way to eat soup (mix them all up J) to our minute day-to-day experiences as mothers.

Finally, I am thankful that God blessed me with my family—Grant, Ralph, and Gaea— and their never-ending love and support. Our family's experiences have informed many of my beliefs and values about race, and I think we are a prime example of how different cultures can make a beautiful reality.

—*Bessie Lawton*

ABOUT THE AUTHORS

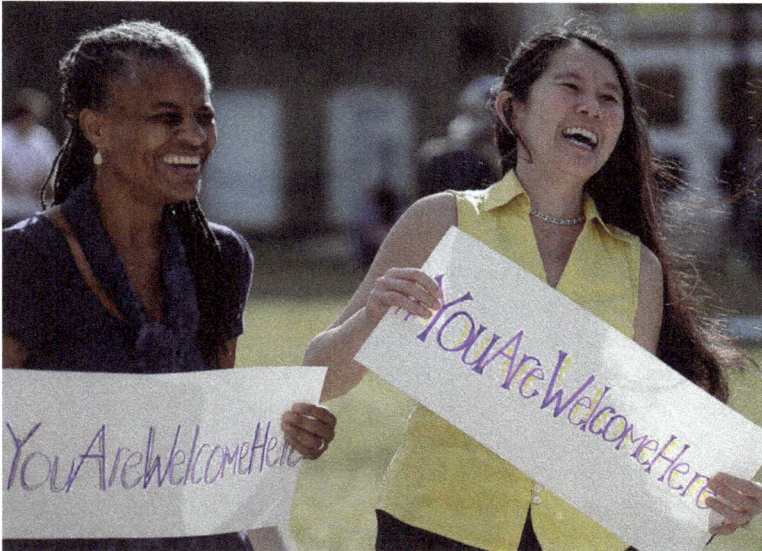

Anita Foeman, Ph.D., is a Professor of Communication and Media at West Chester University. She received her PhD from Temple University in 1982 in Communication with a concentration in Organizational Communication. She was one of the first in her field to publish on diversity in the workplace as a positive development. Her co-authored article "Ethnic Culture and Corporate Culture" published in 1987 articulates a positive image of workplace diversity. Dr. Foeman's ongoing scholarly work explores diversity in society including multicultural organizations, families, and people. Her work includes 30 years of diversity and leadership consulting for educational, government, and private agencies. Her orientation has always been optimistic and incisive. For the past fifteen years, Dr. Foeman's research has examined identity based on ancestry DNA data. Her first publication on this work was "Science and Magic: DNA and the Racial Narratives that Shape the Social Construction of Race in the USA" published in 2006.

This work has been followed by a series of articles and professional presentations including publications in *Communication Monographs, Communication Quarterly,* the journal *Identity* and the open access journal *Genealogy.* Her work has received coverage in the *New York Times,* the *Washington Post, Here & Now* on NPR, the *BBC News Hour, National Geographic Magazine, National Geographic Explorer,* and *NOVA.* She is working on a professional lecture series for the Great Course organization.

Bessie Lee Lawton, Ph.D., is Professor of Communication and Media at West Chester University. She received her Ph.D. from the University of Pennsylvania in 1994, and her MA and BA from the University of the Philippines. She has done research on interracial relationships, portrayals of Native Americans on YouTube, cultural aspects of heritage language learning, and pedagogical issues related to teaching general education courses. Prior to teaching, she worked as Research Analyst for marketing and broadcasting companies both in the United States and in the Philippines, and as Program Officer for international health promotion programs. She also worked as a feature writer for magazines in the Philippines before she came to the United States. Her scholarly work has been published in *Communication Monographs, Howard Journal of Communications, Language, Culture and Curriculum, Gazette, Identity, Journal of Intercultural Communication Research, Journal of Development Communication, Journal of Communication Media Watch, American Indian Quarterly, New Media and Society, Genealogy, Journal of Intercultural Communication, Communication Teacher, E-learning and Digital Media, and Online Journal of Communication and Media Technologies, among others.* Her work with Dr. Anita Foeman has been featured in the New York Times, National Public Radio, and other popular media outlets.

CREDITS

GLOSSARY

Actuarial — Mathematical analysis to calculate insurance risks, premiums, financials. This is done by trying to predict uncertainty, for example one's life expectancy.

Adaptation — Adjusting, often for survival. It generally requires relinquishing some element of what one has done or known.

Africana studies — The interdisciplinary examination of the cultural, political, historical, social, and economic experiences of people of African descent throughout the worldwide African diaspora.

Afrocentrism — An approach to learning that puts Africa at the center of examination. This is different from the approach that makes European and Western culture the standard and center. The "out of Africa" theory of humanity, for example, looks at human history beginning in sub-Saharan Africa.

Anti-miscegenation — Miscegenation is the mixing of what are identified socially as different racial groups generally in marriage, but also in cohabitation, sexual relations, or procreation—any behavior that would seem to dilute the purity of races. Anti-miscegenation laws made such practices illegal.

Assimilation (as in cultural assimilation) — A process wherein one culture comes to be more similar to another. This generally involves giving up parts of the original culture. Assimilation may take the form of changes in behaviors, appearance, language, and other qualities of the assimilating group.

Attitudinal bias — Having a predisposition toward something that is either positive or negative. Bias makes it difficult to be open to new alternate information.

Behavioral discrimination — Refers to negative actions toward others based on prejudices against a particular group. This is different from having negative attitudes toward a group.

Better babies movement — A term that was associated with the eugenics movement with the goal of encouraging some people to reproduce and others not to in order to engineer a high-quality population.

CCD (Confraternity of Christian Doctrine) classes — A religious education program of the Roman Catholic Church generally provided for Catholic youth.

Cisgender — A person whose identity and gender is consistent with the sex attributed to them at birth.

Code switching — The ability to communicate in different ways in different situations. While we all have different ways of talking and acting in different settings, in our meaning, code switching is associated with social survival. An example might be the ability of a Black males to talk in ways that will not make White people uncomfortable.

Colorism — A preference for light skin tone over dark ones. This is not just an individual preference but a global pattern that is associated with colonialism.

Contested identity — Disagreement about what categorization a person can claim. For example, a biracial person might identify as the race of either parent or as mixed. Others may question their right to any of these labels.

Deconstructing race — Exposing, considering, and challenging the assumptions about race in order to understand its impact on individuals and structures in society.

Defining narratives — The stories that are the most important in expressing how we see ourselves and how we fit into society. A story about how our ancestors immigrated to the United States might be such a narrative.

DNA (deoxyribonucleic acid) — A molecule that carries genetic directions for every element of the human body. DNA exists in every cell in the human body.

Dominant culture — The social group that controls resources. As such, it is able to bend those not in power to its cultural standards and will. The power of the dominant culture is often so profound that their characteristics are simply seen as regular or normal, which can make their influence difficult to see.

Dominant White culture — This is generally the culture that is seen as the standard, mainstream, or normal. In many cases it is so influential that people do not even see it as a particular culture, just reality.

Ecological — Relating to the environment.

Ethnicity — Category where we feel belongingness, usually on the basis of national or cultural background or a unique set of life experiences including language and history.

Eugenics — Literally derived from the Greek "good birth" or "good creation." It is the belief that the human population can be improved by encouraging some people to reproduce and discouraging others, often through means including forced sterilization.

External variable — Influences in the environment other than one's genetic makeup. This could include elements like diet or stress.

Fall of Saigon — On April 30, 1975, this event marked the end of the Vietnam War. Communist North Vietnamese and Viet Cong forces captured the South Vietnamese capital of Saigon, forcing the South Vietnamese to concede. Some Vietnamese supporters of the United States escaped to America during this time period.

Financial capital — Having access to funds or other monetary resources.

Gene editing technology — Allows scientists the ability to alter parts of genes, often by removing or adding to them.

Genetic profiling — Examining a person's genetic information to determine certain qualities; these might be visible characteristics or disease predisposition, for example.

Geneticist — Scientist who studies genes, genetic variation, and heredity.

Genogram — A family tree that also includes visual notations of aspects like relationship distance or closeness, sexual identity, relationship status, and so on.

Genome — All of the genetic information that makes up a person.

Genotype — Genetic make-up.

Green card — Identification that one is legally a permanent resident of the United States and can live and work in the United States on an ongoing basis. It is not the same as citizenship.

Group consciousness — Awareness of one's association with a group. That might be a racial or other identity group. Thinking of oneself in terms of the group and not just as an individual. For example, feeling embarrassed if a member of your group does something individually humiliating.

Haplogroup — A group of people of genetic similarity.

Hispanic — A native speaker of Spanish. The person might be from Europe or Latin America, for example. Sometimes people use the term interchangeably with Latinx; however, Latinx generally refers to people of Latin American background.

Holocaust — This is generally a reference to the extermination of more than six million Jews in Germany at the hands of Nazis. Other groups, including sexual and ethnic minorities and the disabled, were also purged. The term can also refer to any mass destruction and is sometimes used to refer to other instances of violent genocide.

Hybridity — A mix. In terms of racial identity, this is one that includes more than one racial group as a blend. For example, a person might identify as biracial.

In vitro fertilization — A medical procedure in which an egg is fertilized by sperm outside the body.

Inbreeding coefficient — The mathematical measure of the probability (between 0 and 100%) that genes at a location in the DNA are identical by descent. In other words, the likelihood that one's immediate ancestors on both sides are direct blood relatives.

Indigenous — The first inhabitants of a location. The term *Native American* (or first Americans or Indigenous Americans) is often used to refer to Indigenous people of the Americas.

In-group — The people we consider part of our identity group. We often have higher and different standards of treatment for those in our in-group than people we consider as outsiders, people in the out-group.

Intersex — A general term used for a variety of circumstances in which a person is born with reproductive or sexual anatomy that doesn't fit the binary of what is seen as typically male or typically female.

Intrapersonal — Within one's self. Intrapersonal communication is communication with yourself. By the way, we all talk to ourselves.

Known narrative — What we know about our background. This may come from direct experience or what we are told by trusted sources. New direct-to-consumer DNA tests are adding information to our narratives.

Latinx — A gender-neutral and nonbinary alternative to Latino or Latina.

Loving v. Commonwealth of Virginia — The 1967 landmark U.S. Supreme Court decision that ruled that laws banning interracial marriage violate the Equal Protection and Due Process Clauses of the 14th Amendment to the U.S. Constitution.

Migration patterns — In human migration, movement of people from one place in the world to another. The out of Africa theory looks at the movement of humans out of Sub-Saharan Africa into the Middle East, Europe, Asia and throughout the planet.

Mitochondrial DNA (or mtDNA) — DNA within the mitochondrial cell. It travels intact from mother to child and is very helpful in ancestry tracking.

Model minority — A stereotype often used to refer to Asian Americans. The generalization is that Asian Americans are hard-working and are passive. The model minority label is often used to imply that other people of color, African Americans and Latinxs especially, should emulate them.

Multiracial (or biracial, etc.) — An identity that includes more than one ancestry line. Although some people identify as biracial or multiracial, many more people have many ancestry lines in their genetic background but do not identify in this way.

Mutations — The natural changes that occur in our genes. It is as if you were copying a paragraph and made mistakes from time to time. In our genes, these "mistakes" can bring about different visible qualities like hair color. These variants are sometimes referred to as SNPs.

Notations — Markings used on a genogram to indicate various qualities. Notations can be made for love, hate, marriage status, and the like.

Objectivity — This concept is generally associated with not having a bias in a given situation and accepting certain external, agreed-on measurable standards. The further we move away from the physical world, the more such standards tend to be cultural (for example what is beautiful or fun). Since these standards generally relate to what the community accepts, objectivity can in some ways be seen as agreed-on subjectivity.

Other — Used as a verb, it means to treat a person in a way that places them outside of the mainstream (for example, to Other someone). As a noun, to call a person an Other is to label or treat them in this way.

Passing — Presenting oneself in public as part of a group not assigned, generally at birth. This was a term often used to refer to African Americans who presented themselves as White. They generally had significant European ancestry but were identified as Black because of formal or informal rules designating anyone with any African ancestry as Black.

Phenotype — Observable characteristics. They might include hair, eye, or skin color and type.

Race — An identity most often based on our geographic origins, often related to our phenotype (how we look).

Racial appropriation — Taking on another person's culture, often profiting from it, and not giving credit. This was especially rampant with Black music in the early days of rock and roll when White musicians imitated Black music and styles and became wealthy while the Black artists languished. Today, the term is debated.

Racial hierarchy — The relationship of cultures to one another in terms of which is more or less advantaged and valued in society.

Rational thinking — An approach to learning that is based on observable facts and what is considered objective truth.

Scientific method — An approach to learning that grows out of the physical sciences. It is based on creating hypotheses and testing them. Systematic observation, measurement, and experiment are important elements. Replication of results is also an important aspect.

Self-categorization — The choice we make ourselves about how we identify. For example, three different people with the same ancestry might consider themselves Black, White, and Latinx, respectively.

SNP (single nucleotide polymorphism) — A variation in a single DNA building block.

SNR *(single nucleotide repeat)* — Repeated sequences that display a high mutation rate.

Social capital — Embodying qualities that are valued in a culture. They might include having certain credentials, speaking effectively, and being seen as attractive or powerful.

Social comparison — Evaluating one group against others in terms of the factors deemed to be important, like income or racial status.

Social contracts — Understandings, often not written anywhere, about what is expected of people in a cultural setting. Groups with lots of power are often able to bend these contracts to their benefit, for example assuming that everyone should always speak English regardless of their first language.

Social hierarchy — The comparative evaluation of groups based on how qualities such as phenotype, styles, and contribution are valued and acknowledged in a culture.

Social identity — The way we are perceived in the cultural context.

Socially constructed — An idea that is accepted as fact because of common agreement. Such a concept might be quite different from one social group to the next or one time period to the another. For example, who is White has changed considerably over generations in the USA.

Stereotypes — Generalizations. They often relate to expectations about people and their behaviors. Stereotypes may come from actual behaviors but are often taken to extremes; for example, everyone in a group is good at math. They also come from judging one culture from the point of view of another one, for example seeing people in a group as too loud.

Sub-Saharan Africa — The part of the African continent south of the Sahara Desert. Human life began in sub-Saharan Africa.

Systematic scrutiny — Careful and methodical examination based on a particular set of standards.

Test-tube babies — A colloquial term used to refer to egg and sperm fertilized outside of the human body.

Trail of Tears — The forcible removal of thousands of Native Americans from their ancestral lands in 1838 and 1839 imposed by the U.S. government. It is called the Trail of Tears because of the devastating impact on these Indigenous people.

U.S. Census — A population count conducted every 10 years by the federal government. The intent is to count every person of any legal status living the United States. On the basis of this information, federal funds are distributed. Questions about race have varied widely over the lifetime of the Census, which began in 1790.

REFERENCES

1,000 Genomes Project Consortium. (2010, October 28). A map of human genome variation from population-scale sequencing. *Nature, 467*(7319), 1061–1073.

23andMe. (n.d.). 23andMe guide for law enforcement. https://www.23andme.com/law-enforcement-guide/

23andMe. (2020). *23andMe privacy highlights.* https://www.23andme.com/about/privacy/

Ainsworth, C. (2018, October 22). Sex redefined: The idea of two sexes is overly simplistic. *Scientific American.* https://www.scientificamerican.com/article/sex-redefined-the-idea-of-2-sexes-is-overly-simplistic1/

Alexander, B. K. (2004). Passing, cultural performance, and individual agency: Performative reflections on Black masculine identity. *Cultural Studies ↔ Critical Methodologies, 4*(3), 377–404. https://doi.org/10.1177/1532708603259680

Alternet. (2015, June 14). Mimicry is not solidarity: Rachel Dolezal and the creation of antiracist White identity. https://www.alternet.org/2015/06/mimicry-not-solidarity-rachel-dolezal-and-creation-antiracist-white-identity/

American Civil Liberties Union. (n.d.). *Summary of laws regarding genetic discrimination.* https://www.aclu.org/other/summary-laws-regarding-genetic-discrimination

American Heart Association. (2011). *Facts, bridging the gap, CVD health disparities.* https://www.heart.org/idc/groups/heart-public/@wcm/@adv/documents/downloadable/ucm_301731.pdf

Ancestry. (n.d.a). *Understanding inheritance.* https://support.ancestry.com/s/article/Understanding-Inheritance

Ancestry. (n.d.b). *Your privacy.* https://www.ancestry.com/cs/legal/privacystatement

Anderson, K. (2006). How well does paternity confidence match actual paternity?: Evidence from worldwide nonpaternity rates. *Current Anthropology, 47*(3). 513–520.

Ashmore, R.D., Deaux, K., & McLaughlin-Volpe. (2004). An organizing framework for collective identity: Articulation and significance of multidimensionality. *Psychological Bulletin, 130*(1), 80–114.

Bar-Haim, Y., Ziv, T., Lamy, D., & Hodes, R. M. (2006). Nature and nurture in own-race face processing. *Psychological Science, 17*(2), 159–163.

Barnett, J. H., & Smoller, J. W. (2009). The genetics of bipolar disorder. *Neuroscience, 164*(1), 331–343.

BBC. (2013, November 26). *FDA bans 23andme personal genetic tests.* https://www.bbc.com/news/technology-25100878

BBC News. (2017, October 31). Russians' DNA taken by for-
    eign agents, Kremlin says. https://www.bbc.com/news/
    world-europe-41816857?ocid=socialflow_twitter

Berger P., & Luckmann T. (1966). *The social construction of reality: A treatise in
    the sociology of knowledge.* Anchor Books.

Bey, M., & Sakellarides, T. (2016). When we enter: The Blackness of Rachel
    Dolezal. *The Black Scholar, 46*(4), 33–48. https://doi.org/10.1080/000642
    46.2016.1227197

Bhatnagar, S., & Aggarwal, R. (2007). Lactose intolerance is common and
    can be diagnosed clinically and treated with simple dietary measures.
    BMJ, 334(7608), 1331–1332.

Blell, M., & Hunter, M. A. (2019). Direct-to-consumer genetic testings red her-
    ring: "Genetic ancestry" and personalized medicine. *Frontiers in Medicine,
    6.* https://doi.org/10.3389/fmed.2019.00048

Bolnick, D. A., Fullwiley, D., Duster, T., Coper, R. S., Fujimura, J.H., Kahn, J.,
    Kaufman, J. S., Marks, J., Morning, A., Nelson, A., Ossorio, P., Reardon, J.,
    Reverby, S. M., & Tallbear, K. (2007). The science and business of genetic
    ancestry testing. *Science, 318*(5849), 399–400.

Bouche, T., & Rivard, L. (2014, September 18). *America's hidden
    history: The eugenics movement.* Scitable. https://www.
    nature.com/scitable/forums/genetics-generation/
    america-s-hidden-history-the-eugenics-movement-123919444/

Brodwin, E. (2019, January 12). Genetic testing is the future of health-
    care, but many experts say companies like 23andMe are doing more
    harm than good. *Business Insider.* https://www.businessinsider.com/
    future-healthcare-dna-genetic-testing-23andme-2018-12

Brown, K. V. (2018, December 19). *Surprise DNA results are turn-
    ing customer-service reps into therapists.* Bloomberg.
    https://www.bloomberg.com/news/features/2018-12-19/
    surprise-dna-results-are-turning-customer-service-reps-into-therapists

Brown, K. V. (2019, January 22). 23andMe just got FDA
    approval for a DNA cancer test. *Time.* https://time.
    com/5510009/23andme-fda-approval-cancer-test/

Brubaker, R. (2016). The Dolezal affair: race, gender and the micropolitics of
    identity. *Ethnic and racial studies, 39*(3), 414–448.

Burr, V. (1995). *An introduction to social constructionism.* Routledge.

Carey, N. (2013). *The epigenetics revolution: How modern biology is rewriting
    our understanding of genetics, disease, and inheritance.* Columbia Univer-
    sity Press.

Centers for Disease Control and Prevention. (2010). *Table 22: Life expectancy
    at birth, at 65 years of age, at 75 years of age, by race and sex: United
    States, selected years, 1900–2007.* https://www.cdc.gov/nchs/data/
    hus/2010/022.pdf

Chaturvedi, N. (2001). Race as an epidemiological determinant—Crudely
    racist or crucially important? *International Journal of Epidemiology, 30,*
    925–927, p. 927.

Chen, J. M., & Hamilton, D. L. (2012). Natural ambiguities: Racial categorization of multiracial individuals. *Journal of Experimental Social Psychology, 48*(1), 152–164. https://doi.org/10.1016/j.jesp.2011.10.005

Chow, K. (1997). Imagining boundaries of blood: Zhang Binglin and the invention of the Han "race" in modern China. In F. Dikotter (Ed.), *The construction of racial identities in China and Japan* (pp. 34–52). University of Hawaii Press.

Citrin, J., & Sears, D. O. (2014). *American identity and the politics of multiculturalism.* Cambridge University Press.

Clarke, T. K., Adams, M. J., Davies, G., Howard, D. M., Hall, L. S., Padmaabhan, S., Murray, A. D., Smith, B. H., Campbell, A., Hayaward, C., Porteous, D. J., Deary, I. J., & McIntosh, A. M. (2017). Genome-wide association study of alcohol consumption and genetic overlap with other health-related traits in UK Biobank (N = 112 117). *Molecular Psychiatry, 22*(10), 1,376–1,384.

Clinton, W. (2000, June 26). *President Clinton: Announcing the completion of the first survey of the entire human genome.* White House Archives. https://clintonwhitehouse3.archives.gov/WH/Work/062600.html

Cohen, J. (2019, August 1). The untold story of the "circle of trust" behind the world's first gene-edited babies. *Science.* https://doi.org/10.1126/science.aay9400

Cohn, D. (2015, June 18). *Census considers new approach to asking about race by not using the term at all.* Pew Research Center. https://www.pewresearch.org/fact-tank/2015/06/18/census-considers-new-approach-to-asking-about-race-by-not-using-the-term-at-all/

Cordova, F. (1983). *Filipinos: Forgotten Asian Americans.* Kendall Hunt.

Crenshaw, K. (1989). Demarginalizing the intersection of race and sex: A Black feminist critique of antidiscrimination doctrine, feminist theory, and antiracist politics. *University of Chicago Legal Forum, 1,* 139–167.

Cross, W., Seaton, E., Yip, T., Lee, R., Rivas, D., Gee, G., Roth, W., & Ngo, B. (2017). Identity work: Enactment of racial-ethnic identity in everyday life. *Identity, 17*(1), 1–12.

DaCosta, K. M. (2007). *Making multiracials: State, family, and market in the redrawing of the color line.* Stanford University Press.

Deaux, K. (2006). *To be an immigrant.* Russell Sage Foundation.

Debunking Denial. (n.d.) *The history of eugenics in America, Part II: Bad blood, the American eugenics movement.* https://debunkingdenial.com/bad-blood-the-american-eugenics-movement/

Defleur, M. L., & Goffman, E. (1964). Stigma: Notes on the management of spoiled identity. *Social Forces, 43*(1), 127–128. https://doi.org/10.2307/2575995

Dikotter, F. (1997). Racial discourse in China: Continuities and permutations. In F. Dikotter (Ed.), *The construction of racial identities in China and Japan* (pp. 12–33). University of Hawaii Press.

DNA Doe Project. (n.d.). *Home.* http://dnadoeproject.org/#

Egorova, Y. (2009). The proof is in the genes? Jewish responses to DNA research. *Culture & Religion, 10*(2), 159–175.

Equal Employment Opportunity Commission. (2008). *The Genetic Informa-tion Nondiscrimination Act of 2008.* https://www.eeoc.gov/laws/statutes/gina.cfm

Estes, R. (2018). *DNA Explained.* https://dna-explained.com/2018/09/13/ancestry-2018-ethnicity-update/

Family History Guide. (n.d.). *Project 7: DNA.* https://www.thefhguide.com/project-7-dna-an.html

FamilySearch. (2018). *Privacy notice (updated 2018-09-01).* https://www.familysearch.org/legal/privacy

Felter, C. (2019, March 12). *Measles and the threat of the anti-vaccination movement.* Council on Foreign Relations. https://www.cfr.org/article/measles-and-threat-anti-vaccination-movement

FindLaw. (n.d.). *Havasupai tribe of Havasupai reservation v. Arizona Board of Regents.* https://caselaw.findlaw.com/az-court-of-appeals/1425062.html

Fisher, W. R. (1985). The narrative paradigm: An elaboration. *Communication Monographs, 52*(4), 347–367.

Fisher, W. R. (1987). *Human communication as narration: Toward a philosophy of reason, value, and action.* University of South Carolina Press.

Fisher, W. R. (1989). *Human communication as narration: Toward a philosophy of reason, value, and action.* University of South Carolina.

Fiske, S. T. (2012). Warmth and competence: Stereotype content issues for clinicians and researchers. *Canadian Psychology, 53*(1), 14–20

Foeman, A. (2009). Science and magic: Using DNA data to examine the social construction of race. *Journal of Intercultural Communication Stud-ies, 18*(2), 14–25.

Foeman, A. (2012). An intercultural project exploring the relationship among DNA ancestry profiles, family narrative, and the social construction of race. *The Journal of Negro Education, 81*(4), 307–318. https://doi.org/10.7709/jnegroeducation.81.4.0307

Foeman, A., & Howard, A. (2014, October). *Experiential learning cycle to the WCU DNA Diversity Project* [Paper presentation]. Knowledge Crossing Borders conference, Heredia, Costa Rica.

Foeman, A., & Lawton, B. (2013, June). *Exploring global identity in education: Ancestry DNA and diversity training as classroom approaches for creating awareness of a global community* [Paper presentation]. Frederick Dou-glass Institute and Ghana Interdisciplinary Conference on Diversity and Culturalism, Cape Coast, Ghana.

Foeman, A., Lawton, B. L., & Rieger, R. (2015). Questioning race: Ancestry DNA and dialog on race, *Communication Monographs, 82*(2), 271–290.

Gaff, C., & Bylund, C. L. (Eds.). (2010). *Family communication about genetics: Theory and practice.* Oxford University Press.

Genesight. (2020). *Genesight psychotropic test.* https://genesight.com/endtrialanderror/?creative=352940689873&keyword=%2Bgene%20

%2Bsite&matchtype=b&network=g&device=c&ads_cmpid=735880026&ads_
adid=42088656607&ads_matchtype=b&ads_net-
work=g&ads_creative=352940689873&utm_term=%2Bgene%20
%2Bsite&ads_targetid=kwd-78193756929&utm_campaign=&utm_
source=adwords&utm_medium=ppc&ttv=2&gclid=Cj0KCQjw2K3rBRDi-
ARIsAOFSW_56epNfEPst65ymOspw-t19fOweQFHENa9AN-
PIBiM3UHOYyL5AK85EaAvNuEALw_wcB

Gerbner, G. (1995). Foreword: What's wrong with this picture? In Yahya R.
Kamalipour (Ed.), *The U.S. media and the Middle East: Image and perception* (pp. xiii–xvi). Praeger.

Goffman, E. (1964). *Stigma: Notes on the management of spoiled identity.*
Penguin.

Golbeck, N., & Roth, W.D. (2012). Aboriginal claims: DNA ancestry testing
and changing concepts of indigeneity. In S. Berthier-Foglar, S. Colling-
wood-Whittick & S. Tolazzi (Eds.) *Biomapping Indigenous peoples: Toward
an understanding of the issues* (pp. 415–432). Rodopi.

Goldenberg, D. (2016). *The curse of ham race and slavery in early Judaism,
Christianity, and Islam.* Princeton University Press.

Gordon, M. (1964). *Assimilation in American life: the role of race, religion and
national origins.* Oxford University Press.

Gratton, B., Gutmann, M. P., & Skop, E. (2007). Immigrants, their children,
and theories of assimilation: Family structure in the United States, 1880–
1970. *The History of the Family: An International Quarterly, 12*(3), 203–222.
https://doi.org/10.1016/j.hisfam.2007.10.003

Gugliotta, G. (2008, July). The great human migration. *Smithsonian Magazine.* https://www.smithsonianmag.com/history/
the-great-human-migration-13561/

Haeusermann T., Fadda, M., Blasimme, A., Tzovaras, B.G., & Vayena, E. (2018).
Genes wide open: Data sharing and the social gradient of genomic privacy. *AJOB Empirical Bioethics, 9*(4), 207–221.

Hales, C. M., Carroll, M. D., Fryar, C. D., &. Ogden, C. L. (2017). Prevalence of
obesity among adults and youth: United States, 2015-2016. *NCHS Data
Brief, 288.*

Hall, M. J., Reid, J. E., Burbidge, L. A., Pruss, D., Deffenbaugh, A. M., Frye, C.,
Wenstrup, R. J., Ward, B. E., Scholl, T. A., & Noll, W. W. (2009). BRCA1 and
BRCA2 mutations in women of different ethnicities undergoing testing
for hereditary breast-ovarian cancer. *Cancer, 115*(10), 2,222–2,233.

Haney-López, I. (2006). *White by law 10th anniversary edition: The legal construction of race.* New York University Press.

Harkins, G. (2019, July 3). *Mail-in ancestry DNA kits may help enemy to target
you, Navy's top officer says.* Military.com. https://www.military.com/
daily-news/2019/07/03/mail-ancestry-dna-kits-may-help-enemy-tar-
get-you-navys-top-officer-says.html

Hecht, M. L. (1993). A research odyssey: Towards the development of a Communication Theory of Identity. *Communication Monographs, 60*(1), 76–82.

Hecht, M. L., Jackson, R. L., & Pitts, M. J. (2005). Culture: Intersections of intergroup and identity theories. In J. Harwood & H. Giles (Eds.), *Intergroup communication: Multiple perspectives* (pp. 21–42). Peter Lang.

Hecht, M. L., & Lu, Y. (2014). Communication theory of identity. In T. L. Thompson (Ed.), *Encyclopedia of health communication* (pp. 225–227). SAGE.

Herper, M. (2013, November 25). 23andStupid: Is 23andMe self-destructing? *Forbes*. https://www.forbes.com/sites/matthewherper/2013/11/25/23andstupid-is-23andMe-self-destructing/#63cc165611c0, para. 9–10.

Hickman, C. B. (1997). The devil and the one drop rule: Racial categories, African Americans, and the U.S. Census. *Michigan Law Review, 95*(5), 1161–1265. https://doi.org/10.2307/1290008

Hirschman, E. C., & Panther-Yates, D. (2008). Peering inward for ethnic identity: Consumer interpretation of DNA test results. *Identity: An International Journal of Theory and Research, 8*(1), 47–66.

History.com Editors. (2019, May 14). *U.S. immigration timeline*. History.com https://www.history.com/topics/immigration/immigration-united-states-timeline

Ho, A. K., Kteily, N., & Chen, J. M. (2017). "You're one of us": Black Americans' use of hypodescent and its association with egalitarianism. *Journal of Personality and Social Psychology, 113*(5), 753–768.

Hochschild, J. L., Burch, T. R., & Weaver, V. M. (2012). *Creating a new racial order: How immigration, multiracialism, genomics, and the young can remake race in America*. Princeton University Press.

Hofstede Insights. (2019). *Philippines*. https://www.hofstede-insights.com/country/the-philippines/

Hsu, M. Y. (2017). *The good immigrant: How the yellow peril became the model minority*. Princeton University Press.

Ignatiev, N. (1995). *How the Irish became White*. Routledge.

Ingelsson, E., & Knowles, J. (2017). Leveraging human genetics to understand the relation of LDL cholesterol with Type 2 diabetes. *Clinical Chemistry, 63*(7), 1187–1189.

The Innocence Project. (n.d.). *Exonerate the innocent*. https://www.innocenceproject.org/exonerate/

Ioannidis, J. P. (2005). Why most published research findings are false. *PLOS Medicine, 2*(8), e124.

Jackson, R. L. (2002). Cultural contracts theory: Toward an understanding of identity negotiation. *Communication Quarterly, 50*(3–4), 359–367. https://doi.org/10.1080/01463370209385672

Johnson, C. (2008). The end of the Black American narrative. *American Scholar, 77*, 32–42.

Jones, J. H. (1993). *Bad blood: The Tuskegee syphilis experiment*. The Free Press.

Jordan, S. (2016). *A critical race perspective on the Filipino identity*. UC Berkeley: Summer Undergraduate Research Fellowship Conference Proceedings. https://escholarship.org/uc/item/4877f5z0

Joseph, A. (2017, October 23). *A baby with a disease gene or no baby at all: Genetic testing of embryos creates an ethical morass.* Statnews. https://www.statnews.com/2017/10/23/ivf-embryo-genetic-testing/

Jung, E., & Hecht, M. L. (2004). Elaborating the communication theory of identity: Identity gaps and communication outcomes. *Communication Quarterly, 52*(3), 265–283.

Kaylin, J. (2006). *The virus behind the cancer.* Yale Medicine. https://medicine.yale.edu/news/yale-medicine-magazine/the-virus-behind-the-cancer.aspx

Kendler, K. S., Jacobson, K. C., Prescott, C. A., & Neale, M. C. (2003). Specificity of genetic and environmental risk factors for use and abuse/dependence of cannabis, cocaine, hallucinogens, sedatives, stimulants, and opiates in male twins. *American Journal of Psychiatry, 160*(4), 687–695.

Keyton, J. (2005). *Communication and organizational culture.* SAGE.

Kiang, L., & Takeuchi, D. T. (2009). Phenotypic bias and ethnic Identity in Filipino Americans. *Social Science Quarterly, 90*(2), 428–455. https://doi.org/10.1111/j.1540-6237.2009.00625.x

Kingstone, L. S. (2018). *Fading out black and white racial ambiguity in American culture.* Rowman & Littlefield.

Koerner, A., LeRoy, B., & Vaetch, P. (2010). Family communication. In C. Gaff & C.L. Bylund (Eds.), *Family communication about genetics: Theory and practice patterns* (pp.184–198). Oxford University Press.

Kohn, D. (2014). *Millions of Americans changed their racial and ethnic identity from one census to the next.* Pew Research Center.

Kolata, G. (2017, April 6). FDA will allow 23andMe to sell genetic tests for disease risks to consumers. *New York Times.* https://www.nytimes.com/2017/04/06/health/fda-genetic-tests-23andme.html

Kopacz, M., & Lawton, B. L. (2011). The YouTube Indian: Portrayals of Native Americans on a viral video site. *New Media and Society, 13*(2), 330–349.

Kopacz, M., & Lawton, B. L. (2013). Talking about the YouTube Indian: Images of Native Americans and viewer comments on a viral video site. *Howard Journal of Communications, 24*(1), 17–37.

Krogstad, J. M., Passel, J. S., & Cohn, D. (2019, June 12). *5 facts about illegal immigration in the U.S.* Pew Research Center. https://www.pewresearch.org/fact-tank/2019/06/12/5-facts-about-illegal-immigration-in-the-u-s/

Kubick, W. (2013). Personalized medicine, data, and me: Is it time to realize the extraordinary promise and vision of personalized medicine? *Applied Clinical Trials, 22*(10). http://www.appliedclinicaltrialsonline.com/personalized-medicine-data-and-me

Lawton, B., & Foeman, A. (2017). Shifting winds: Using ancestry DNA to explore multiracial individuals' patterns of articulating identity. *Identity, 17*(2), 69–83.

Lawton, B., Foeman, A., Arevalo, D., & Brown, L. (2008). Coping strategies for interracial couples making decisions about children's education. *Iowa Journal of Communication, 40*(2), 155–179.

Lawton, B., Foeman, A., & Surdel, N. (2018). Bridging discussions of human history: Ancestry DNA and new roles for Africana Studies. *Genealogy, 2*(5), 1–10. https://doi.org/10.3390/genealogy2010005

Lawton, B. L., & Logio, K. (2009). Teaching the Chinese language to heritage versus non-heritage learners: Parents' perceptions of a community weekend school in the United States. *Language, Culture, & Curriculum, 22*(2), 137–155.

Lerner, A. B. (2015, June 15). Rachel Dolezal sued Howard University for discrimination. *Politico.* https://www.politico.com/story/2015/06/rachel-dolezal-sued-howard-university-119024

Lin, M. H., Kwan, V. S. Y., Cheung, A., & Fiske, S. T. (2005). Stereotype content model explains prejudice for an envied outgroup: Scale of anti-Asian American stereotypes. *Personality and Social Psychology Bulletin, 31*(1), 34–47.

Lombardo, P. A. (2008). *Three generations, no imbeciles: Eugenics, the Supreme Court, and Buck v. Bell.* Johns Hopkins University Press.

Lopez, I. (1994). The social construction of race: Some observations on illusion, fabrication, and choice. *Harvard Civil Rights-Civil Liberties Law Review, 1*(62), 6–7, 11–17.

Loving v. State of Virginia, 388 U.S. 1 (1967)

Lwin, S. (2006). A race so different from our own: Segregation, exclusion, and the myth of mobility. In H. Raphael-Hernandez & S. Steen (Eds.), *AfroAsian encounters: Culture, history, politics* (pp. 17–33). New York University Press.

Mandal, A., Leger, R., Graham, L., Ishimwe, N., Vitale, A., Innocent, N., Hodges, B, & Mandal, P. (2015). An overview of human genetic disorders with special reference to African Americans. *Journal of Bioprocessing and Biotechniques, 5*(10), 1–3.

Marcus, H.R., Steele, C.M., & Steele, D.M. (2000). Colorblindness as a barrier to inclusion: Assimilation and nonimmigrant minorities. *Journal of the Academy of Arts and Sciences*, 129(4), 233-259.

Martin, P., Hagestad, G. O., & Diedrick, P. (1988). Family stories: Events (temporarily) remembered. *Journal of Marriage and the Family, 50*(2), 533–554.

McCarthy, V. P., Bartels, D. M., & LeRoy, B. S. (2007). Coming full circle: A reciprocal-engagement model of genetic counseling practice. *Journal of Genetic Counseling, 16*(6), 713–728. https://doi.org/10.1007/s10897-007-9113-4

McCoskey, D. E. (2012). *Race: Antiquity and its legacy.* I.B. Tauris.

McGoldrick, M., Gerson, R., & Petry, S. (2008). *Genograms: Assessment and intervention* (3rd ed.). Norton.

Merikangas, K. R., Stlar, M., Stevens, D. E., Goulet, J., Preisig, M. A., Fenton, B., Zhanga, H., O'Malley S. S., & Rounsaville, B.J. (1998). Familial transmission of substance abuse disorders. *Archives of General Psychiatry, 55*(11), 973–979.

Mizrahi, K. (2005). *Americans' attitudes toward immigration and immigrants: The role of values, social identification, and attitudinal ambivalence.* City University of New York.

Molteni, M. (2018a, June 1). GEDMatch and DNA phe-noytyoping. *Wired.* https://www.wired.com/story/police-will-crack-a-lot-more-cold-cases-with-dna/

Molteni, M. (2018b, August 3). 23andMe's pharma deals have been the plan all along. *Wired.* https://www.wired.com/story/23andMe-glaxosmithkline-pharma-deal/

Molteni, M. (2019, April 27). The creepy genetics behind the Golden State killer case. *Wired.* https://www.wired.com/story/detectives-cracked-the-golden-state-killer-case-using-genetics/

Moody Investor's Service. (2018). *Credit implications differ for life and health insurers impacted by genetic testing technology.* https://www.moodys.com/research/Moodys-Credit-implications-dif-fer-for-life-and-health-insurers-impacted--PR_385943

Mukherjee, S. (2016). *The gene: An intimate history.* Scribner.

MyHeritage. (2020). *MyHeritage privacy policy.* https://www.myheritage.com/privacy-policy

Nakayama, T. K., & Krizek, R. L. (1995). Whiteness: A strategic rhet-oric. *Quarterly Journal of Speech, 81*(3), 291–309, https://doi.org10.1080/00335639509384117

National Academies of Sciences, Engineering, and Medicine. (2017). *The economic and fiscal consequences of immigration.* National Academies Press.

National Center for Biotechnology Information. (n.d.). *How to: Find genes associated with a phenotype or disease.* https://www.ncbi.nlm.nih.gov/guide/howto/find-gen-phen/

National Congress of the American Indian (NCAI) & American Indian and Alaska Native Genetics Resource Center. (n.d.). *Havasupai Tribe and the lawsuit settlement aftermath.* https://tribalclimateguide.uoregon.edu/literature/havasupai-tribe-and-lawsuit-settlement-aftermath

National Public Radio. (2007, December 5). *Transcript: JFK's speech on his religion.* https://www.npr.org/templates/story/story.php?storyId=16920600

Nelson, S. S. (2000). An Ethnic Strategy on the Census. The LA Times. https://www.latimes.com/archives/la-xpm-2000-apr-17-me-20574-story.html

Ocampo, A. C. (2016). *The Latinos of Asia: How Filipino-Americans break the rules of race.* Stanford University Press.

Oikkonen, V. (2015). Mitochondrial Eve and the affective politics of human ancestry. *Signs Journal of Women in Culture and Society, 40*(3), 747–772 https://doi.org/10.1086/679527

Osalbo, J. G. (2011). *Filipino American identity development and its relation to heritage language loss* [Unpublished master's thesis, California State University, Sacramento, CA].

Oveyssi, N. (2015, July 7). *Forgotten stories of the eugenics age #1: How "better babies" become "fitter families."* Center for Genetics and Society. https://www.geneticsandsociety.org/biopolitical-times/forgotten-stories-eugenic-age-1-how-better-babies-became-fitter-families

Panofsky, A., & Donavan, J. (2017). *When genetics challenges a racist's identity: Genetic ancestry testing among White nationalists.* https://osf.io/preprints/socarxiv/7f9bc/

Park, R. E. (1928). Human migration and the marginal man. *American Journal of Sociology, 33*(6), 881–893. https://doi.org/10.1086/214592

Payne, A. (2017, March 28). *Rachel Dolezal on Rihanna, her DNA test, "fraud" claims and other Facebook questions.* NBC News. https://www.nbcnews.com/news/nbcblk/rachel-dolezal-rihanna-her-dna-test-fraud-claims-other-facebook-n739331

PBS. (n.d.). *Go deeper: Race timeline.* https://www.pbs.org/race/000_About/002_03_c-godeeper.htm

Phelan, J. C., Link, B. G., & Feldman, N. M. (2013). The genomic revolution and beliefs about essential racial differences: A backdoor to eugenics? *American Sociological Review, 78*(2), 167–191.

Phelan, J., Link, B., Zelner, S., & Yang, L. (2014). Direct-to-consumer racial admixture tests and beliefs about essential racial differences. *Social Psychology Quarterly, 77*(3), 296–318.

Phillips, A. M. (2016). Only a click away—DTC genetics for ancestry, health, love ... and more: A view of the business and regulatory landscape. *Applied & Translational Genomics, 8*, 16–22.

Portes, A., & Zhou, M. (1994). Should immigrants assimilate? *Public Interest, 116*, 18–34.

Radford, J., & Noe-Bustamente, L. (2019). *Facts on U.S. Immigrants, 2017, statistical portrait of the foreign-born population in the United States.* Pew Research Center. https://www.pewresearch.org/hispanic/2019/06/03/facts-on-u-s-immigrants-2017-data/

Rasmussen. (2015, June 22). *Most Black voters don't think Rachel Dolezal should have resigned from NAACP.* https://m.rasmussenreports.com/public_content/politics/general_politics/june_2015/most_black_voters_don_t_think_rachel_dolezal_should_have_resigned_from_naacp

Regalado, A. (2019, February 21). China's CRISPR twins might have had their brains inadvertently enhanced. *MIT Technology Review.* https://www.technologyreview.com/2019/02/21/137309/the-crispr-twins-had-their-brains-altered/

Renn, K. A. (2004). *Mixed race students in college: The ecology of race, identity, and community.* SUNY Press.

Renn, K. A. (2008). Research on biracial and multiracial identity development: Overview and synthesis. *New Directions for Student Services, 2008*(123), 13–21. https://doi.org10.1002/ss.282

Richeson, J. A., & Sommers, S. R. (2016). Toward a social psychology of race and race relations for the Twenty-First century. *Annual Review of Psychology, 67,* 439–463. https://doi.org/10.1146/annurev-psych-010213-115115

Risch, N., Burchard, E., Ziv, E., & Tang, H. (2002). Categorizations of humans in biomedical research: Genes, race, and disease. *Genome Biology, 3*(7), 1–12.

Rosenblum, M. R., & Ruiz Soto, A. G. (2015). *An analysis of unauthorized immigrants in the United States by country and region of birth.* Migration Policy Institute. https://www.migrationpolicy.org/research/analysis-unauthorized-immigrants-united-states-country-and-region-birth

Roth, W. D., & Ivemark, B. (2018). Genetic options: The impact of genetic ancestry testing on consumers' racial and ethnic identities. *American Journal of Sociology, 124*(1), 150–184.

Rutherford, A., & Mukherjee, S. (2017). *A brief history of everyone who ever lived: The human story retold through our genes.* The Experiment.

Saul, S. (2005, June 24). FDA approves a heart drug for African-Americans. *New York Times.* https://www.nytimes.com/2005/06/24/health/fda-approves-a-heart-drug-for-africanamericans.html

Sautman, B. (1997). Myths of descent, racial nationalism and ethnic minorities in the People's Republic of China. In F. Dikotter (Ed.), *The construction of racial Identities in China and Japan* (pp. 75–95). University of Hawaii Press.

Schizophrenia Working Group of the Psychiatric Genomics Consortium. (2014). Biological insights from 108 schizophrenia-associated genetic loci. *Nature, 511*(7510), 421–427.

Schmidt, J. (2018). Emma, Carrie, Vivian: How a family became a test case for forced sterilizations [Podcast]. *WUWM* https://www.wuwm.com/post/emma-carrie-vivian-how-family-became-test-case-forced-sterilizations#stream/0

Schrijver, I., Pique, L., Graham, S., Pearl, M., Cherry, A., & Kharrazi, M. (2015). The spectrum of CFTR variants in nonWhite cystic fibrosis patients: Implications for molecular diagnostic testing. *The Journal of Molecular Diagnostics, 18*(1). http://dx.doi.org/10.1016/j.jmoldx.2015.07.005

Scientific American. (2009, May 1). The need to regulate "designer babies." https://www.scientificamerican.com/article/regulate-designer-babies/

Shih, M., & Sanchez, D. T. (2009). When race becomes even more complex: Toward understanding the landscape of multiracial identity and experiences. *Journal of Social Issues, 65*(1), 1–11.

Skloot, R. (2010). *The immortal life of Henrietta Lacks.* Crown.

Smart, A., Bolnick, D. A., & Tutton, R. (2017). Health and genetic ancestry testing: Time to bridge the gap. *BMC Medical Genomics, 10*(1), 3. https://doi.org/10.1186/s12920-016-0240-3

Spreckels, J., & Kotthoff, H. (2009). Communicating identity in intercultural communication. In H. Kotthoff & H. Spencer-Oatey (Eds.), *Handbook of intercultural communication* (pp. 415–440). Mouton de Gruyter.

Stets, J., & Burke, P.J. (2000). Identity theory and social identity theory. *Social Psychology Quarterly, 63*(3), 224–237.

Stone, E. (2017). *Black Sheep and Kissing Cousins: How Our Family Stories Shape Us.* Routledge.

Stonequist, E. V. (1935). The problem of the marginal man. *American Journal of Sociology, 41*(1), 1–12.

Sudmant, P. H., Mallick, S., Nelson, B., Hormozdiari, F., Krumm, N., Huddleston, J., & Eichler, E. (2015). Global diversity, population stratification, and selection of human copy number variation. *Science, 349*(6253), 1–23. https://doi.org/10.1126/science.aab3761

Suzuki, B. H. (2002). Revisiting the model minority stereotype: Implications for student affairs practice and higher education. *New Directions for Student Services, 97*, 21–32.

Sykes, B. (1998). *The seven daughters of Eve.* Oxford University Press.

Sykes, B. (2002). *The seven daughters of Eve: The science that reveals our genetic ancestry.* Norton.

Sykes, B., & Irven, C. (2000). Surnames and the Y chromosome. *The American Journal of Human Genetics, 66*(4), 1417–1419. https://doi.org/10.1086/302850

Tajfel, H., & Turner, J. C. (2004). The social identity theory of intergroup behavior. In J. T. Jost & J. Sidanius (Eds.), *Political psychology: Key readings* (pp. 276–293). Psychology Press.

Taylor, K. (2019, October 3). Parents paid to open college doors. Now they're spending to limit prison time. *New York Times.* https://www.nytimes.com/2019/10/03/us/college-admissions-scandal-consultants.html

Tebas, P., Stein, D., Tang, W. W., Frank, I., Wang, S. Q., Lee, G., Spratt, S. K., Surosky, S. T., Giedlin, M. A., Nichol, G., Holmes, M. C., Gregory, P. D., Ando, D. G., Kalos, M., Collman, R. G., Binder-Scholl, G., Plesa, G., Hwang, W.-T., Levine, B. L., & June, C. H. (2014). Gene editing of CCR5 in autologous CD4 T cells of persons infected with HIV. *New England Journal of Medicine, (370)*10, 901–910.

Tierney, J. (1988, January 11). The search for Adam and Eve. *Newsweek, 111.* https://i.b5z.net/i/u/736324/i/IN_SEARCH_FOR_ADAM___EVE.pdf

U.S. Census Bureau. (2012). *Census Bureau releases results from the 2010 Census Race and Hispanic Origin Alternative Questionnaire Research.* https://www.census.gov/newsroom/releases/archives/2010_census/cb12-146.html

U.S. National Library of Medicine. (n.d.). *Help me understand genetics: Inheriting genetic conditions.* https://ghr.nlm.nih.gov/primer

Waddington, C. H. (1957) *The strategy of the genes.* Macmillan.

Wailoo, K. (2012). Who am I? Genes the problem of historical identity. In K. Wailoo, A. Nelson, & C. Lee (Eds.), *Genetics and the unsettled past: The collision of DNA, race, and history* (pp. 13–19). Rutgers University Press.

Wald, P. (2008). Blood and stories: How genomics is rewriting race, medicine, and human history. In S. L. Gilman (Ed.) *Race in contemporary medicine* (pp. 1–31). Routledge.

Wang, W. (2012, February 16). *The rise of intermarriage.* Pew Research Center http://www.pewsocialtrends.org/2012/02/16/the-rise-of-intermarriage/

Weiland, S., & Geertz, C. (1982). The interpretation of culture and the culture of interpretation. *College English, 44*(8), 784–797. https://doi.org/10.2307/377331

Wells, S. (2006). *Deep ancestry: Inside the Genographic Project.* National Genographic Society.

Whorf, B. L. (1940). Science and linguistics. *Technology Review, 42,* 229–231.

Wikipedia. (2020). *Rachel Dolezal.* https://en.wikipedia.org/wiki/Rachel_Dolezal

Wilkinson, S. (1998). Study abroad from the participants' perspective: A challenge to common beliefs. *Foreign Language Annals, 31,* 23–39.

Witherspoon, D., Wooding, S., Rogers, A., Marchani, E., Watkins, W., Batzer, M., & Jorde, L. (2007). Genetic similarities between and within human populations. *Genetics, 176*(1), 351–359. https://doi.org/10.1534/genetics.106.067355

Wolinsky, H. (2011). Genomes, race and health. Racial profiling in medicine might just be a stepping stone towards personalized health care. *EMBO Reports, 12*(2), 107–109. https://doi.org/10.1038/embor.2010.218

Wong, A. (2018, June 19). Harvard's impossible personality test. *The Atlantic.* https://www.theatlantic.com/education/archive/2018/06/harvard-admissions-personality/563198/

World Bank. (2019). *Fertility rate, total (births per woman).* https://data.worldbank.org/indicator/SP.DYN.TFRT.IN

Yep, G. A. (2002). Navigating the multicultural identity landscape. In J. N. Martin, T. K. Nakayama, & L. A. Flores (Eds.), *Readings in cultural contexts* (pp. 60–66). McGraw-Hill.

Yong, E. (2018, December 3). The CRISPR baby scandal gets worse by the day. *The Atlantic.* https://www.theatlantic.com/science/archive/2018/12/15-worrying-things-about-crispr-babies-scandal/577234/

Yoon, D. H., & Chin, G. J. (2020). *Chinese Exclusion Act of 1882.* Encyclopedia.com. https://www.encyclopedia.com/history/united-states-and-canada/us-history/chinese-exclusion-act

Zack, N. (2003). Race and philosophic meaning. In B. Boxill (Ed.), *Race and racism* (pp. 43–57). Oxford University Press.

Zeitlin, S. J., Kotkin, A. J., & Baker, H. C. (1982). *A celebration of American family folklore: Tales and traditions from the Smithsonian collection.* Pantheon.

Zhang, S. (2018, July 18). Big pharma would like your DNA: 23andMe's $300 million deal with GlaxoSmithKline is just the tip of the iceberg. *The Atlantic.* https://www.theatlantic.com/science/archive/2018/07/big-pharma-dna/566240/

Zhou, M. (2007). Are Asian Americans becoming "White?" *Contexts, 3*(1), 29–37.

INDEX

"The Search for Adam and Eve,"
(Tierney), 129
The Strategy of the Genes
(Waddington), 165
Tierney, John, 129
Trail of Tears, 134
"transracial person," 111
trust, historical breaches of, 143–145
Tuskegee Syphilis Study, 153–154
23andMe, 136, 149–150, 152

U

United States
immigrants role of race in, 49–55
intensity of race in, 51–52
racial intolerance against African
Americans, 55
racial narrative of, 78
United States Public Health Service
(PHS), 154
University of Oxford, 96
U.S. Census, 71, 79

W

Waddington, Conrad Hal, 165

Wald, Priscilla, 145
Weaver, Vesla, 41, 116
wellness
direct-to-consumer DNA
information supporting,
135–139
Wells, Spencer, 20
West Chester University, 153
White nationalists, 10–11, 73
Whorf, Benjamin Lee, 13
Wilkinson, Sharon, 65
Wise, Tim, 123
Wojcicki, Anne, 135

Z

Zack, Naomi, 9
Zhang, Sarah, 151

www.ingramcontent.com/pod-product-compliance
Lightning Source LLC
Chambersburg PA
CBHW050435280326
41932CB00013BA/2128